INSTITUTE OF LEADERSHIP & MANAGEMENT

SUPER SERIES

Networking and Sharing Information

FOURTH EDITION

Published for the
Institute of Leadership & Management by

Pergamon *Flexible* **Learning**

OXFORD   AMSTERDAM   BOSTON   LONDON   NEW YORK   PARIS
SAN DIEGO   SAN FRANCISCO   SINGAPORE   SYDNEY   TOKYO

Pergamon Flexible Learning
An imprint of Elsevier Science
Linacre House, Jordan Hill, Oxford OX2 8DP
200 Wheeler Road, Burlington, MA 01803

First published 1986
Second edition 1991
Third edition 1997
Fourth edition 2003

British Library Cataloguing in Publication Data
A catalogue record for this book is available from the British Library

ISBN 0 7506 5885 1

For information on Pergamon Flexible Learning
visit our website at www.bh.com/pergamonfl

Institute of Leadership & Management
registered office
1 Giltspur Street
London
EC1A 9DD
Telephone 020 7294 3053
www.i-l-m.com
ILM is part of the City & Guilds Group

The views expressed in this work are those of the authors and do
not necessarily reflect those of the Institute of Leadership &
Management or of the publisher

Author: Dela Jenkins
Incorporating some previous material by Howard Senter, Joe Johnson,
    Elaine Horrocks and Diana Thomas
Editor: Dela Jenkins
Editorial management: Genesys, www.genesys-consultants.com
Composition by Genesis Typesetting Limited, Rochester, Kent
Printed and bound in Great Britain by MPG Books, Bodmin

Contents

Contents

Workbook introduction

1 ILM Super Series study links

This workbook addresses the issues of *Networking and Sharing Information*. Should you wish to extend your study to other Super Series workbooks covering related or different subject areas, you will find a comprehensive list at the back of this book.

2 Links to ILM Qualifications

This workbook relates to the following learning outcomes in segments from the ILM Level 3 Introductory Certificate in First Line Management and the Level 3 Certificate in First Line Management.

C2.3   Briefing Skills
1. Select relevant information prior to briefing
2. Plan and prepare effective briefings
3. Conduct effective briefings
4. Adopt appropriate communication methods for feedback to management.

C2.6   Information Awareness
1. Appreciate the importance of using physical senses to absorb data on activities and behaviour
2. Actively listen, and disregard distractions

3   Use observation and perception to gather relevant data
4   Recognize non-verbal cues
5   Interpret data to provide information to forecast developments.

C1.7   Networking
1   Understand the value of networking to self, others and organization
2   Identify people internal and external to the organization and why they are valuable contacts
3   Manage networking relationships that are valuable to all parties involved.

3 Links to S/NVQs in Management

This workbook relates to the following elements of the Management Standards which are used in S/NVQs in Management, as well as a range of other S/NVQs.

D1.1   Gather required information
D1.2   Inform and advise others

It will also help you to develop the following Personal Competences:

■ acting assertively;
■ communicating;
■ influencing others;
■ searching for information.

4 Workbook objectives

Winston Churchill was a remarkable leader. All through the Second World War people across the United Kingdom would huddle round their wireless sets listening to his speeches. He seemed to understand how ordinary people were feeling, their fears of invasion, their anxiety about loved ones away fighting the enemy. He was able to use that understanding, that 'empathy', to inspire his fellow citizens to keep fighting with a determination that, in the end, won the War.

Churchill's skills at oratory are legendary. Such phrases as "We will fight them on the beaches' still live on in people's memories, but where did he acquire the skill to deliver such a powerful message? Most people are surprised to learn that he had a speech impediment, and hated public speaking and shook with fear at the thought of it.

Speaking in public is high on most people's list of things they dread most. The image of all those faces staring at us and waiting for a brilliant display of rhetoric is enough to make us weak at the knees.

But it needn't be like that. By following a few simple rules and, like Churchill, doing a great deal of practice, you can master the skills needed to communicate confidently and with authority.

Session A of this workbook helps you to develop your communication skills so that you will be able to deliver clear and effective briefings to members of your team and others in your work environment.

One of Churchill's many abilities was to 'tune in' to the mood of the nation. He understood intuitively the feelings and emotions of those around him, and knew how to respond to them. This ability to communicate at the subconscious level is the subject of Session B. You will learn how to deduce what people are thinking and feeling from the way they behave, the way they speak and, often, the hidden messages underlying what they say.

However good you are at communicating at the conscious or subconscious level, you can't be sure that you know all you need to know about every subject you are involved in. Session C looks at ways in which you can build a network of people with the experience and knowledge you need to achieve your objectives both in the workplace and outside it.

4.1 Objectives

When you have completed this workbook you will be better able to:

- prepare and deliver effective briefings to your team, and contribute to briefings given by others;
- use your senses to gather information from those around you;
- use the technique of whole body listening to pick up hidden messages;
- explain the value of networking, and create a network to promote both your work objectives and social interests.

An effective briefing will often involve the creation and delivery of a visual presentation of your information and so this is also tackled in this workbook.

5 Activity planner

You may decide to look at the following activities now so that you can prepare for them in advance.

- For Activity 4 (page 7) you need to enlist a friend or colleague to listen to a short briefing you have prepared.
- Activity 13 (page 20) requires you to attend a briefing given by someone else.
- Activity 20 (pages 29–30) requires you to make a video recording of a briefing you have prepared.
- Activity 32 (pages 52–53) asks you to enlist the help of a friend or colleague to carry out an exercise in communicating.
- Activities 42, 43, 44 and 45 (pages 72–76) ask you to choose, plan and research a knowledge network.

Activities 6 to 9 (pages 10–13), Activity 20 and Activities 42 to 45 may provide the basis of evidence for your S/NVQ portfolio. All Portfolio Activities and the Work-based assignment are sign-posted with this icon.

The icon states the elements to which the Portfolio Activities and Work-based assignment relate.

The Work-based assignment (on page 87) will require that you spend time gathering information and agreeing the task with your manager and workteam. You might like to start thinking about whom you should approach, and perhaps arrange a time to chat with them, to gather any information you need.

Session A
Successful briefings and presentations

1 Introduction

A rumour had been circulating all afternoon that something was about to happen. People were getting nervous. Then word went round that everyone should congregate in the programming team's work area. There was going to be a briefing. The contractors weren't sure whether they were included as well as the permanent staff, but they went anyway.

Neil, the team leader, cleared his throat and, with his eyes fixed firmly on the floor, announced that their project had been cancelled and there would be redundancies. That was all he could say until more details had been decided. Everyone spent the rest of the afternoon in little worried huddles, wondering what was going to happen next.

This was a bad experience for everyone involved, and they all blamed Neil. Indeed, he had very little going for him – no hard facts, no backup from his superiors, no good news to soften the blow. But even in this extreme situation he could have handled the situation much better.

In this session you will learn how to present information – whether good or bad – so that everyone will come away from the briefing with an understanding of your message and a feeling that they have been fully informed.

2 The purpose of briefings and presentations

The main purpose of briefings and presentations is to:

■ give information out;
■ get information back.

There are several situations in which you may have to give a briefing or presentation, for example:

■ telling your team about some change that will effect them – as Neil was attempting to do in the example above;
■ getting all team members to share information about their work in progress;
■ informing a group of visitors about some aspect of your work;
■ updating senior managers on team progress.

Activity 1

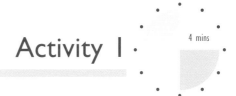

4 mins

What briefings or presentations have you attended recently, either as the presenter of the information or as part of the audience? List three of them.

_____

_____

_____

Briefings and presentations can be a pleasure, a necessity, a chore, a nuisance or a test, depending on the circumstances.

They can seem like a waste of valuable time. They certainly take up time; many briefings are badly organized and poorly run. They can be inconclusive and frustrating. Depending on your past experience, you may strongly dislike them.

But briefings and presentations are a fact of every manager's life; the point is to learn to make them work, and not to hold too many because, if they are seen as time-wasters, they will lose their impact and people will eventually not even bother to attend.

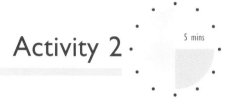

Activity 2

5 mins

Think back to some of the less successful briefings and presentations you have attended in the past. Write down five or six words that describe what you felt was wrong with them.

_____

_____

_____

You may have suggested that they were too long, they dealt with trivia, you couldn't hear all that was said, they were badly presented or they concerned matters that were irrelevant to your own work.

However, a briefing or presentation doesn't have to be like that. It can be efficient, productive and even enjoyable as long as you:

■ prepare for it carefully;
■ ensure that your audience is also prepared;
■ conduct it effectively.

3 Which medium?

Briefings can be delivered verbally or in writing.

3.1 Verbal briefings and presentations

Formal verbal briefings and presentations are highly structured, and communication is often more one way than it is in an informal briefing. Examples include:

- presentations given to external groups to explain the activities of your work area;
- regular 'tool box talks' to your team members about some aspect of their work.

Informal verbal briefings are usually briefings which you give to your team when you want to:

- bring about changes of attitude or behaviour;
- co-ordinate team actions;
- explain something new.

Every time you brief members of your team you are also effecting the way they relate to one another. Since these are working relationships, this incidental aspect of communication is important.

Even the most casual and 'off the record' chat can help to:

- mould attitudes;
- strengthen team spirit;
- show you and the team members where you stand in relation to one another.

Activity 3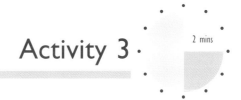

2 mins

David calls his team together and explains that the Chief Executive Officer (CEO) of the whole corporate group will be visiting the site tomorrow.

What purpose does this briefing serve?

_____

_____

What effects is it likely to have on the team's working relationships?

_____

_____

There are two purposes behind this simple communication: an **open** agenda and a **hidden** agenda.

The open agenda is about practical objectives – in this case to inform the team members about the CEO's visit so that they will be prepared for it.

The hidden agenda is about feelings and attitudes – keeping the team informed encourages trust and team spirit. It also helps the individual team members to feel more involved in events, and hence more empowered.

If David's communication hits its target, the world is changed in three small but useful ways:

- the team members possess some information they didn't have before;
- they have the choice to take action, for example, to tidy their desks;
- their confidence in the team leader is strengthened.

The meaning of this for you as a manager should be obvious. When you speak to your team members:

- you often do so in order to achieve a particular objective;
- you always affect the way they relate to you.

If you brief your team well, you can strengthen bonds, create loyalty, build morale and improve productivity. If you brief them poorly, or not enough, the opposite can happen.

3.2 Written briefings

Written communication is usually much more formal than verbal communication.

To see the difference, you only need to write down word for word what someone says. It will usually look very disjointed in print.

In the last few years more and more written briefings have been distributed in the form of emails. They can range from being one-line reminders to long-winded communications that most people tend to ignore. It is left up to the recipients whether to download them to a pc or to print them out. There is usually no way that the sender can tell that the message has been received.

The advantage of writing is that we usually have longer to absorb it. Spoken words are gone almost instantly.

In general, it is preferable to communicate in writing when the briefing:

- is a short, non-controversial message (often sent via email);
- is long and relatively complicated;
- contains background information and supporting documentation;
- doesn't involve changing the team members' attitudes or feelings.

The rest of this session will concentrate on the skills required to give verbal briefings, although most of the rules also apply to written ones.

4 Selecting information

In selecting the information to present at your briefing session or presentation, you need to think about the following questions:

- what sort of people are in my audience?
- what are the **key** facts and feelings I want to pass on to them, i.e. what are my objectives?
- what do they know already?
- what are their current attitudes and feelings?

How much do you know about your audience? If they are your team members, then you probably have a pretty good idea about how much they know and feel. If they are visitors to the organization or members of another department, you can't assume very much at all. If this is the case, there are three simple rules for what you say and how you say it:

- don't assume your listeners know as much as you do;
- don't use language they might not understand;
- don't give them too much information too quickly.

4.1 Don't make assumptions

Activity 4

15 mins

You need a colleague or friend to help in this Activity – someone who is not an electrical specialist. Ask him or her to sit quietly and listen carefully. Then slowly read out this extract from a technical lecture.

'As the magnets rotate, a pole passes the ignition chargecoil, which generates a current through the rectifier RI. This charges up the capacitor to a voltage of, say, 350 volts; the magnet rotates further and generates a pulse of electrical energy in a "pulse coil". The coil is movable around the stator, so that timing may be adjusted. The energy pulse passes through the rectifier R2 to the gate of the thyristor, whereupon the thyristor conducts, and the stored electrical energy in the capacitor gives a high, short-duration current through the ignition coil primary. The secondary voltage produces a plug spark in which the "rise time" is extremely short, a condition which will make the plug work well, even though it may have an incorrect gap or be partly fouled. You can think of this sudden discharge as punching a way through the plus fouling salt deposits. Note the absence of a contact breaker in this form of CDI.'

Now ask your colleague these three questions:

1   What is this passage describing?

2   How is the capacitor charged?

3   How can the timing be adjusted?

If your colleague answers the questions correctly, it will be a remarkable performance. The vast majority of people would not be able to (unless they made detailed notes) because:

■   there is too much information;
■   too much of it is new;
■   it is too complex;
■   it uses technical language with which most people would not be familiar.

Any listener who can make sense of it must:

■   already have a lot of knowledge of the subject;
■   understand technical jargon such as 'stator' and 'rise time'.

Do you only brief people who know as much about your subject as you do? Probably not. Often your listeners will be other first line managers and their teams, trainees, visitors and people from other departments.

4.2 Information overload

> First tell them what they MUST know, then what they SHOULD know, and finally, and only if you have the time, what they COULD know.

A speaker who overloads the audience with information is wasting everybody's time. All listeners have a limit: they can soak up what they hear, but only so much and only so fast.

In practice, if you give your listeners too much information too quickly:

- some of it will not get through at all;
- some of it will get through in a mangled or muddled state;
- you will have no idea what has got through correctly and what hasn't;
- if you really overdo it, your audience may give up listening altogether.

Activity 5 · 3 mins

Given the example in Activity 4 and the comments above, how can you avoid giving your listeners information overload? Make a note of at least **five** things you can do.

_____

_____

_____

_____

_____

Answers can be found on page 100.

If you follow these rules, you will benefit in two ways:

- you will need to say less;
- more of it will get through.

4.3 Dealing with sensitive issues

When you are selecting the material for your briefing or presentation, keep in mind the impact it might have on your audience. It is always useful to be forewarned of any opposition that might arise during your briefing. In sensitive situations (such as announcements of cut-backs or work re-organization), use your contacts to find out who might be particularly hostile as well as who might be particularly friendly.

Once you have identified such people you can try to help the situation by:

- sending round papers or memos explaining your case;
- using your network to discover the nature of their objections;
- lobbying – explaining your case and asking for support on a one-to-one basis;
- doing deals – agreeing to support another person's case in return for their supporting yours.

Your preparatory work will help you to put over your argument at the meeting itself.

Note: you will learn more about networking in Session C.

5 Planning and preparation

If you have prepared your briefing or presentation thoroughly, you will have every reason to feel confident when you actually give it. But you must be prepared to put in the effort – most speakers find that they **spend at least five times longer preparing a briefing than they actually spend giving it**.

A well tried formula for preparing a briefing is as follows:

Step	Action
1	Draft the objectives
2	List the content
3	Design the structure
4	Prepare visual aids and demonstrations
5	Have a rehearsal

Let's look at each step in detail.

5.1 Step 1: Draft the objectives

Think about your purpose, the needs of your listeners and the context in which you will be giving the briefing. Ask yourself:

- what is the purpose of the briefing or presentation?
- who will be listening?
- where will I be doing the briefing or presentation?

When you are clear about the answers to these questions, write down your objectives for the briefing, i.e. what you want the audience to be able to do as a result. For example:

> Suppose you have to give a briefing to a group of local secondary school teachers who are considering placing work-experience students with your organization. They want to know what it is like to work in your team, and the sort of work you actually do. The briefing will take place at the Teachers' Centre, and you will have up to 15 minutes altogether, plus a little time for questions.

Your main objective might be:

'by the end of the briefing the secondary school teachers will be able to accurately describe the work done by my team'.

5.2 Step 2: List the content

Decide the key points you need to put across to your audience in order to achieve your objectives.

Activity 6   10 mins

S/NVQ D1.2

Using a separate sheet of paper make a list of the key points you would want to make. This Activity may provide the basis of appropriate evidence for your S/NVQ portfolio.

5.3 Step 3: Design the structure

Work out a sensible and logical structure for the points you are going to make. This should consist of:

- an introduction;
- a main part;
- an end (summary and conclusions).

Always design the main part first.

Main part

This is where you expand and explain the key points listed in step 2. For example, if your first point is that your organization has 'a reputation for quality', you may want to support that by stating:

- who thinks so;
- what you mean by quality;
- why it is considered important;
- what you do to maintain it.

Let's work out a way of putting down the content of a briefing, using the example already given above. Look back at the details of the briefing to the teachers outlined in section 5.1.

Now let's look at how you can develop the main message.

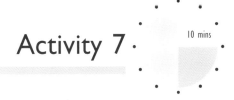

Activity 7

10 mins

S/NVQ D1.2

This Activity, together with Activities 8 and 9, may provide the basis of appropriate evidence for your S/NVQ portfolio.

Look back to your response to Activity 6 and, building on that, think again carefully about what you need to say. If you need to change anything, do so. Then write down on a separate sheet of paper the main points again in logical order as briefly as you can. Choose no more than **eight** key points.

When you are happy with your list of key points, write each one at the top of a blank sheet of paper or large index card. These will be the skeleton of your briefing.

Now you need to go through the process of refining each key point to include everything else you need to mention. The result will be a list of subsidiary points under each key point.

Activity 8 ·

10 mins

S/NVQ D1.2

This Activity, together with Activities 7 and 9, may provide the basis of appropriate evidence for your S/NVQ portfolio.

Consider each of your key points in turn and list under each one the subsidiary points, making sure you put them in logical order.

For example:

KEY POINT	I	A REPUTATION FOR QUALITY
SUBSIDIARY POINTS	1.1	Operating at quality end of the market
	1.2	Customers are very demanding (reject anything not to highest standard)
	1.3	Competition intense; quality keeps customers loyal
	1.4	Highly skilled workforce
	1.5	Have made big investment in training (give examples)
	1.6	Rigorous inspection at every stage

You now have a complete skeleton of the main part of your briefing, written out in logical order on separate sheets or cards. This simple outline can be the basis of the visual aids that you will produce later.

Introduction, summary and conclusion

Activity 9 · 10 mins

S/NVQ D1.2

This Activity, together with Activities 7 and 8, may provide the basis of appropriate evidence for your S/NVQ portfolio.

1 Take a clean sheet of paper or index card and head it INTRODUCTION.

If you start by drafting the main body of the briefing, the introduction, summary and conclusion will practically write themselves.

2 Below that write down, as briefly as you can, the various things you need to say in your introduction to the teachers.

For example:

> ### INTRODUCTION
>
> Good morning, etc.
>
> My name is . . . . .
>
> I am a first line manager at . . . .
>
> We produce control systems
>
> Up-to-date, high tech, forward looking
>
> Stop me if there is anything
>
> Happy to answer questions afterwards.

3 Now use new sheets or cards to do the same for the summary and conclusion.

The conclusion needs a little thought. Think about what this particular group of listeners needs to know, for example:

■ your attitude to work experience students;
■ what will be expected of them;
■ what the students can expect to gain from the experience.

Activity 10

Look at the following examples of introductions and conclusions and jot down whether you think each of them is good, or not, and why you think so.

1   'Well, I – um – as you know, I haven't done much of this speaking so I – um – can't promise to do anything too amazing. But, as I've been called on to say a few words about my section – component assembly – well here goes. . .'

_____

_____

2   'For the last six months we have been working (25 hours a day sometimes) on the Delta project. As the section team leader, I'd like to explain a bit about...'

_____

_____

3   'I am delighted to have the chance to share with you some of the good news we have had lately on the progress of the migration project. As you know, I am not one to boast about the achievements of my team, but I can't help pointing out. . .'

_____

_____

4   'Well, I think that's about all . . .Yes, I think so. That's it then.'

_____

_____

5   'So the main thing is for us to keep up the same level of work in the next financial year. And for that we need your support. Thank you.'

_____

_____

You may have said something along the following lines.

Speaker 1

Bad. Listening to this, you might sympathize with his nervousness, but you wouldn't be impressed. If you say you're not going to be any good, listeners will tend to believe you. Don't apologise for yourself. By the time you stand up to speak you are committed, so you might as well make the best of it.

This speaker is rather slow to get going. We don't know anything about what he is going to talk about, only that the self-confidence to do it is lacking. It would be better to get to the point straight away as Speaker 2 does.

Speaker 2

Good. The speaker gets to the point straight away and makes a slight joke ('25 hours a day sometimes') to establish a friendly relationship with the listeners.

Speaker 3

Good. This gets to the point in a friendly way and immediately gets listeners on the speaker's side 'I am delighted to . . .share with you. . .').

The performance is confident – the speaker makes a slight joke of the fact that she never boasts – and doesn't apologise for herself.

Speaker 4

Not very good. In the same way as you don't want to start to speak with an apology for yourself, so you don't want to finish by just letting your subject peter out. You can throw away a good, well-organized briefing by such a feeble ending. This is why it is often useful to include in your notes exactly what you want the last line to be. Quite frequently, your listeners won't even know that you have missed out part of what you intended to say if you finish with a flourish.

Speaker 5

Good. This is much better than Speaker 4. The speaker repeats the main point of the speech very briefly ('the main thing for us is to keep up the same level of work. . .') and leaves his listeners in no doubt about what is wanted from them.

And, having finished, the speaker stops – without any vague remarks about this being the end.

Notice, too, that the speaker thanks the listeners at this point. If you feel it is appropriate to thank your audience for their response, then this is the time to do it – at the end.

Don't worry about the odd 'um' and 'er' – that's something everybody does.

So we can now draw up a checklist of do's and don'ts to bear in mind when you come to do the briefing:

- don't apologise for yourself;
- do get to the point as soon as possible;
- don't just peter out – finish firmly;
- do thank your audience at the end if this is appropriate;
- if you are rattled, don't show it – just pause and take your time to sort it out;
- show them you're in charge, and do what has to be done: that's what the audience expects.

5.4 Step 4: Prepare visual aids and demonstrations

Visual aids

**I hear and I forget.
I see and I remember.**

There are excellent reasons for using diagrams, slides, models or other equipment that will help your listeners get the message because:

- they help your listeners to remember the points you are making;
- they make the whole presentation more interesting and credible;
- some things are easier to communicate visually than verbally.

Activity 11

4 mins

What kinds of visual aid would be useful in a briefing about your own work? Note down **four** different kinds.

_____

_____

_____

_____

Every situation will be different, but you could think about how to show the audience:

- what the working environment is like (slides, photos, perhaps a video);
- what the 'end product' is (actual examples, models, photos);
- what the work you do consists of (diagrams, charts, samples);
- how the workload, output, etc. has progressed (diagrams, charts).

Visual aids don't have to be graphical, of course. One of the most useful things to do is to 'flash up' your key points in writing as you go along – on a flipchart, as slides for an overhead projector (OHP) or as a projected 'PowerPoint' demonstration.

For example, if your first key point is 'This company has always had a reputation for quality', you could present it on the OHP or flipchart page like this:

> **A reputation for quality**

You could then keep that point on view until you are ready to make the next point. Alternatively you could put all your points on one sheet or slide and talk through them one by one.

EXTENSION 1
This extension gives you a brief guide to using overhead projectors and other visual aids.

Visual aids are extremely useful but they need careful preparation, so make sure you allow yourself enough time. Good visual aids can make your presentation go better, but if they are torn, scruffy, smudged or hard to see, it will go worse.

Before you begin your presentation, remember to check that:

- all your visual aids are ready;
- the equipment is set up and working properly.

Demonstrations

> **I hear and I forget.**
> **I see and I remember.**
> **I do and I understand.**

Sometimes, if you are doing a team briefing, you might want to demonstrate rather than just talk. For example, a new method for disposing of waste packing materials might involve you in:

- walking the team round the site, and pointing out examples of good and bad practice;
- demonstrating how to use a machine designed to compress waste into bundles – a potentially dangerous machine.

There is a standard formula for this kind of briefing:

I	Introduce the subject and describe what is required.
2	Explain why.
3	Explain when the new procedure is to be used.
4	Demonstrate how to carry out the procedure.
5	Ask team members to do it for themselves.
6	Correct and advise them where necessary.
7	Check understanding and competence.
8	If necessary, repeat steps 4 to 7.

5.5 Step 5: Have a rehearsal

You should now have a set of up to ten sheets or cards, most of which should not have very much written on them, and a set of visual aids.

Most of the hard work is behind you. You have created a framework for the briefing. You now need to decide how exactly you are going to deliver it.

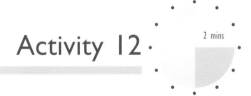

Activity 12

Some speakers prefer to write out their speech in full and then read it word for word. This is perhaps because they feel there is less risk of making a mistake. Note down one disadvantage of doing this.

If you just read out a full script:

■ it is likely to sound very artificial (it's difficult to write speech in a natural way);

■ your eyes will be focused on the paper most of the time (so you can't see the signals the people in the audience are sending you – such as smiles, nods of the head, and so on);

- it will be difficult to establish 'rapport' – a two-way relationship – with the audience. When you have rapport you can keep the audience interested and carry them with you. And, equally, you can see what they are thinking and how well you are getting through to them. If necessary, you can adjust what you are saying.

So it is probably best to just keep your notes in front of you and use them simply to jog your memory from time to time. However, if you are going to use this approach, you need to be thoroughly familiar with what you are going to say – and that means practice.

So you need to practise your delivery and make sure than you know how long you will take, how fast to go, and what words to use.

Particularly if you are tackling an important briefing for the first time, it would be worth planning a really thorough programme of practice and rehearsal. You could plan it along the following lines:

	Step	**Action**
I	Private practice	Practise in private, using your notes, and practising any demonstrations you are going to include.
2	Record and play back	Record the whole briefing on audio cassette, then play it back to see how it sounds. Re-record it until you are happy with it.
3	Private audition	Asks colleagues, friends or family members to be the audience, and deliver the briefing to them; ask them what they think, how natural it sounded, whether it was too fast, too slow, too complicated, etc.
4	Dress rehearsal	Using your notes again, rehearse it fully, complete with visual aids and demonstrations.

And finally. . .

if you want to check that your own briefing is going to cover all the key elements needed for success ask yourself these five questions.

- Is it clear what the briefing is about?
- Is it clear who is involved?
- Is it clear why the subject of the briefing is important?
- Is it clear what is expected of the audience after the briefing?
- Is it clear how the audience can get further information?

A lot of work?

Perhaps, but it will be worth it!

Activity 13 · 10 mins

In order to carry out this activity you will need to attend at least one briefing session or presentation given by someone else. If you are not normally invited to such events ask your manager to obtain permission for you to do so.

The aim is to observe and comment on how the person giving the briefing or presentation has planned and structured it. Watch and listen throughout the event and take notes.

Afterwards write a short description of how the speaker:

■ introduced the briefing or presentation and got started;
■ structured the subject matter to ensure that all important points were covered in the time available;
■ ensured that everyone had the opportunity to ask questions at appropriate points;
■ summed up at the end of the briefing.

Score the speaker out of ten for each of these four points, and explain briefly what the problems were, if any.

6 Conducting the briefing or presentation

Now let's look at what really matters to you – the briefing or presentation itself.

6.1 Getting the message across

First line manager, Raj, to team member, Cathy:

'Er, are you busy right now? What I mean is, is what you're doing really urgent…of course it is. I know it's all important…only these orders ought to go out tonight if possible. Could you try and fit them in? Perhaps when you've finished the others? OK, then, I'll leave it with you…'.

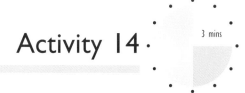

Activity 14

3 mins

What do you think the outcome of the above briefing will be?

How effective do you think the briefing is?

There may have been some kind of feedback confirming that the orders will be sent out tonight. Cathy might have smiled and nodded, or given the thumbs up. But on the face of it we don't know – and neither does Raj.

This is a very poor briefing:

- Raj obviously wants the orders to 'go out tonight', but fails to give a clear instruction to that effect;
- he clearly lacks assertiveness;
- he seems to lack authority.

In practice this is a recipe for trouble. Raj may believe that he has made it clear that the orders are urgent; Cathy's understanding, however, is that it is up to her to decide. Tomorrow, if it turns out that the orders didn't go, there may be a row.

Activity 15

10 mins

Which of the following would be good techniques for making sure that your message gets across?

1	Repeat the central message at least once.
2	Speak loudly and clearly.
3	Keep it short and simple.
4	Be assertive rather than aggressive.
5	Use words and phrases that you are confident the team members will understand.
6	Check that they understand.
7	Use eye contact.

Numbers 1, 3, 5 and 6 are all excellent rules for effective communication. The others need some comment.

| 2 | Speak loudly and clearly. |

It is always better to speak clearly. Speaking loudly may be useful in a noisy environment, or when the audience is spread over a large area. However, in ordinary situations it may make you sound like a school teacher talking to a class of six-year-olds.

| 4 | Be assertive rather than aggressive |

Assertiveness is usually good: it means making it clear what you want without being vague and without being aggressive. Aggressiveness always provokes a bad reaction and damages relations between people.

| 7 | Use eye contact. |

Make eye contact with as many people in the audience as possible, looking from one to another in turn as you speak. Stay focused on each one for a few seconds.

6.2 Speaking with confidence

To 'sell' an idea you have to 'sell' yourself.

You can't help but admire people who stand up confidently in front of a room of strangers and deliver a riveting and polished speech. It seems as though they must have been born with natural energy and confidence.

How come they are so good at it? How come they don't tremble and stutter with nerves? How do they manage to make everything they say seem so important and convincing?

It is tempting to think that they are a totally different kind of person from you – that they really are 'born public speakers'.

However, there is no such thing as a 'born public speaker'. Effective speaking is something of which we are all capable, but which we have to learn. It is simply not true that people who regularly speak in public have had that skill from birth.

So what makes them different? Only three things:

- they are determined to do it well;
- they have learned the necessary communication skills;
- they have practised a lot.

6.3 Dealing with nerves

Communicating with a group can be much harder than communicating with an individual because:

- the fact that there is an audience may put more pressure on you – especially if you are inclined to be nervous or self-conscious;
- it is a more complex task – there are more people to take account of;
- groups behave differently from the individuals who compose them – groups may take on a personality of their own.

All this means that you are under more pressure when dealing with a group, and may feel anxious. Anxiety is the body's automatic reaction to a situation in which it believes that it is facing a serious threat. People who are anxious show it in a number of physical ways.

> Over a pint in the pub Jenny was telling her friends about the traumatic day she had been through at the call centre where she worked. She had been making a presentation to a group of visiting Japanese businessmen on the call-handling system used by her team.

'I was terrified. My head was sort of swimming, and somehow I couldn't see properly – everything was a blur. My heart was thumping away like mad. I started off in a great rush and gabbled like an idiot. My voice was all wobbly and I kept having to swallow because my throat was so dry.

'Then when I had settled down a bit I suddenly realised that my left leg was trembling uncontrollably, and I thought everyone must be able to see it. I lost my place, stuttered and started sweating all over. I don't really know how I got through to the end.

When I'd finished I just wanted to run away and hide. I thought I'd be the laughing stock of the whole department. But the funny thing was that no one seemed to notice, and my manager actually said 'Well done, Jenny – but take it a bit slower next time you do it.' Next time! I couldn't go through that again.'

The reaction of fear or anxiety is natural in such a situation. But you can learn to deal with it by:

■ learning to control your physical reactions;
■ managing your thinking processes;
■ improving your speaking techniques, and thus your self-confidence.

We have already had a quick look at speaking techniques, but it is worth spending a bit of time on the other two areas.

6.4 Controlling your physical reactions

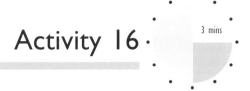

Activity 16

3 mins

Think for a moment of somebody you have heard giving a speech, who you realized was nervous. Perhaps it was somebody at work, at a wedding or on television.

Jot down what signs the speaker gave that he or she was nervous.

Well, the ways of showing nervousness are endless. But common signs include:

- blushing;
- fiddling nervously with tie, cufflinks, jewellery, hair, papers;
- frequent throat-clearing;
- perspiring;
- trembling hands;
- voice too high-pitched, or not coming out at all.

Here are some simple hints for coping with the physical symptoms of anxiety:

- give yourself time: walk a few metres to where you are going to speak;
- spend a few seconds arranging your papers before you start;
- clench your fists very tightly, and then relax them as slowly as you can, several times;
- do breathing and voice control exercises;
- learn relaxation techniques.

6.5 Managing your thinking processes

The problem with having a fear of speaking in front of other people is that it can become a self-fulfilling prophesy. If you think that something bad will happen, it will.

The best way to reduce your fear of speaking in public is to increase your confidence that you **can** do it competently.

> Jeremy had worked for a utility company for ten years. He was the acknowledged expert on the company's electricity billing system, and if anyone had a problem, they naturally turned to Jeremy. So it seemed a great idea when the Director of Training and Development asked him to take on the training role in his section.
>
> But then the panic set in. Jeremy had felt perfectly comfortable briefing his colleagues on a one to one basis. But the thought of standing up in front of eight or ten people and delivering a formal briefing filled him with dread. It reminded him of the time he had toasted the bridesmaids at his wedding – when he had forgotten what he was going to say, and had had to sit down to the cheers and laughter of the guests.
>
> That bad experience had made Jeremy dread any form of speaking in public. He broke out in a sweat just thinking about it.

The good news is that, by learning to manage his thinking processes, Jeremy could change that memory from a nightmare into something positive.

Once you have experienced something it becomes a memory which is stored in your mind. When Jeremy reacted to the memory of his wedding, he was in fact reacting to the way the memory was stored in his mind – as a dark, threatening, terrifying ordeal. And it was this that was making him dread the future training sessions.

Good memories are usually remembered as bright, clear images, possibly in colour, perhaps a bit larger than life, and associated with feelings of warmth and well-being. In contrast, bad memories may appear dull, colourless, indistinct and a bit distant.

Anne, one of Jeremy's colleagues, had just attended a course on neuro-linguistic programming – the study of the relationship between thinking, language and behaviour, i.e. and how people can learn to choose the ways they think, feel and behave. Anne explained, that, according to NLP, Jeremy could learn to 'manage' his memories so that they were stored in a way that resulted in his feeling the way he would like to feel.

> You will learn more about neuro-linguistic programming in Sessions B and C.

With Anne's help, Jeremy learned to see his wedding speech as a warm, funny experience in which his friends were laughing **with**, rather than **at**, him.

When he eventually gave his first briefing, he felt the same warmth and good feeling that he – now – remembered having on his wedding day.

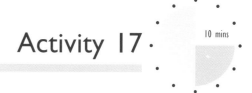

Activity 17

10 mins

Think of a part of your work that you really enjoy. What do you see? What do you hear? What do you feel?

_____

_____

_____

Now think of a part of your work that you don't enjoy very much at all. In what way do you see, hear, feel it differently from the part you enjoy?

If you can reprogramme your bad memory so that it is stored as a bright, 'good-feeling' memory, then it will give you strength and confidence to handle similar situations in the future.

7 When it's all over

After the briefing or presentation is over, you may well heave a sigh of relief and think you can forget all about it. No chance.

Activity 18

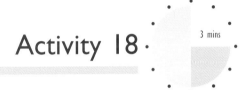
3 mins

What else do you think is left to be done?

There is no point in going through an experience like this if lessons aren't learnt from it.

■ Your manager and other relevant people need to be informed of any significant points that were raised during the briefing or presentation, and any action which should be taken as a result.

■ You need to carry out an evaluation (a kind of post mortem) to judge how well you did and what you could do better next time.

Let's look at each of these in a bit more detail.

7.1 Reporting back to management

As soon as the briefing or presentation is over you should make short notes of:

- what you covered;
- how the audience reacted;
- any significant points raised and, if necessary, how you answered them;
- any further action that needs to be taken.

You could send this in the form of a memo to your manager. Not only will it raise awareness of anything important that happened, but it will also remind your manager of your professional approach to the task you have been given.

7.2 Evaluating your performance

No one does a perfect briefing session or presentation first time round, because learning to speak effectively takes experience as well as preparation. As a beginner, you should be more than satisfied if you have been able to cover the content thoroughly in the time available.

But when you have a few competent performances under your belt, it is time to think about polishing up your act.

Activity 19   8 mins

Think back to the last few times you listened to someone giving a presentation or briefing. Think about how they delivered it, especially their behaviour. In what ways could they have improved their performance?

_____

_____

_____

_____

Some speakers are too technical, too quiet or too monotonous, but there can also be a problem caused by annoying habits and mannerisms. These irritate the audience and distract them from the speech itself. Here are some of the most common ones:

- irritating verbal mannerisms:

  - using catch phrases such as 'to be perfectly honest with you', or 'at the end of the day';
  - saying 'y'know', 'er' and 'well' every few words: 'Well, er, it's, well, got a very good, y'know, reputation for, er, quality. Well...';
  - clearing your throat nervously before each sentence;
  - muttering under your breath when changing a visual aid or doing a demonstration: 'OK, right ... OHP slide on ... right ... there we are ... right';

- irritating non-verbal mannerisms:

  - turning and talking to a flipchart instead of facing the audience;
  - facing the audience but never raising your eyes to look anyone in the face;
  - only looking at one person in the audience during the whole briefing;
  - continually walking back and forth in front of the audience;
  - fiddling constantly, for instance by clicking a pen cap on and off;
  - constantly moving your hands: waving around, in and out of your pockets, picking something up from the table, putting it down again, scratching your head, back in your pockets, up again to rub your nose.

There are many more bad habits like these – and they are almost all subconscious. People simply don't realise that they are doing them.

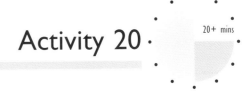

Activity 20

20+ mins

S/NVQ D1.2

This Activity may provide the basis of appropriate evidence for your S/NVQ portfolio. If you are intending to take this course of action, it might be better to write your answers on separate sheets of paper.

Think very hard about your own verbal and physical mannerisms when speaking in public. Ask people who have watched you talking in some formal situation or when the pressure has been on you for some other reason.

If possible, arrange for someone to video you, and watch the tape together afterwards.

Now write down your mannerisms, as honestly as you can. Note which were most likely to distract or irritate an audience.

_____

_____

_____

_____

_____

_____

Now practise speaking without these mannerisms. It's usually best to tackle them one at a time, making sure you've eliminated each one before going on to the next.

Of course, an occasional gesture to emphasize a point is fine, but anything beyond that will get in the way of your message, making you less professional than you could be.

Finally, here is a very straightforward task for you: sit down and watch the television news.

- Watch the newsreaders carefully:
  - they are cool, calm, controlled and restrained;
  - they scarcely ever use a physical gesture, and they avoid irritating mannerisms.

- Listen to them carefully:
  - the words they use are always simple and straightforward;
  - they speak clearly and without hurrying;
  - they've learned to use small changes in the tone and pitch of their voice to fit the 'story', whatever it is.

Watch and listen carefully, because these are the professionals. Most people will never reach such dizzy heights, but it is always worth remembering that once they were just like everyone else. The only difference is that they have worked hard at it, practised their techniques and learned from long experience.

It is all a matter of learning the skills. They did it, and so can you.

8 Changing sides – being a contributor

As a first line manager you will inevitably be required to attend briefings and presentations given by other people.

When you attend a briefing or presentation, there are various reasons why you might be called upon to make a contribution. You might:

- be responsible for providing further information on a topic in your specialist area;
- ask questions;
- provide answers to other people's questions.

So it is not enough just to turn up and leave all the work to the person giving the briefing or presentation.

As a member of the audience you share responsibility for the success of the event.

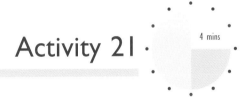

Activity 21

4 mins

What can the audience do to make sure a briefing or presentation goes well? Suggest two or three ideas.

You could have said that the audience should:

- listen attentively;
- use encouraging body language;
- ask relevant questions.

To put it simply, everyone who is being addressed should take a positive and constructive attitude and support the briefer's objective of trying to get through the briefing or presentation session in the time allowed with everything explained and understood.

A passive or hostile attitude, which often comes from people who 'hate briefings', certainly won't improve matters.

It also helps if the members of the audience:

- study any relevant documents beforehand;
- only ask questions at appropriate points in the briefing;
- keep any contributions short and to the point.

There are three reasons why you should try to make good quality contributions to a meeting:

- it will help the briefing or presentation to work better and produce better outcomes;
- you are more likely to achieve the outcomes you are personally seeking;
- it will improve your personal reputation and help your career.

Activity 22 · 3 mins

Write down six words that would describe a good quality contribution.

_____   _____

_____   _____

_____   _____

You probably listed words like 'relevant', 'coherent', 'brief', 'powerful', 'well-informed', 'well-argued', and so on. Actually the measure of quality is when listeners think to themselves 'That made a lot of sense', showing that the message got though and was both understandable and credible.

Self-assessment 1

20 mins

1   What is the hidden agenda that is part of all briefings and presentations?

_____

_____

2   I _____ and I forget.

I see and I _____.

I do and I _____.

3   When you are preparing to argue a case, you should find out the nature of any objections to it beforehand. Why?

_____

_____

4   What causes anxiety?

_____

5   The structure of a briefing or presentation always consists of three distinct parts. What are they?

_____

_____

_____

6   Complete these sentences outlining three excellent reasons for using visual aids:

a   Some things are easier to _____ visually than in speech.

b   Visual aids help your listeners to _____ the points you are making.

c   Visual aids make the whole presentation more _____ and _____.

7 What are the eight steps in carrying out a demonstration?

8 What four questions should you ask when selecting information to include in a briefing or presentation?

9 What do we mean when we say a speaker has 'rapport'?

Answers to these questions can be found on pages 97–8.

9 Summary

- When you brief or give a presentation to your team:

  - you usually do so in order to achieve a particular objective;
  - but it always affects your working relationship with them.

- An effective briefing or presentation has outcomes that change the world in small but useful ways.

- A briefing or presentation is a two-way process in which your attention to feedback is crucial. It always pays to check that the messages have got through in the way you intended.

- For an effective briefing or presentation:

  - repeat the central message at least once;
  - speak clearly and assertively;
  - keep it short and simple;
  - use words and phrases that you are confident the team members will understand;
  - check that they do understand;
  - use visual aids to supplement your verbal messages;
  - speak calmly and at a gentle pace;
  - limit the amount of information you try to communicate.

- Planning a formal briefing should cover the following stages:

  - working out your objectives;
  - deciding the key points of the content;
  - working out a structure;
  - preparing appropriate visual aids and demonstrations;
  - practising and rehearsing.

- Using visual aids and demonstrations makes the briefing more interesting and the messages more memorable.

- In the briefing or presentation, your introduction, summary and conclusions are of major importance. You should plan them carefully.

- Body language plays a big role in communication. Make sure that it doesn't distract from or contradict your message.

- After the briefing or presentation is over you should make a report to your manager and carry out an evaluation of your performance.

- You should be prepared to contribute to briefings and presentations made by others and help make these a success.

Session B
Active listening

1 Introduction

Don and Angela were first line managers in a woollen mill. One day all managers in the company were called to a briefing by the CEO. He announced that a major new Icelandic range was about to be introduced which would enable the company to recover its share of the international wool market. The new range would replace certain other product lines that were being discontinued, and he was sure that, in next three months, they would be re-hiring many of their former staff to handle the additional work load.

Walking back to their department after the briefing, Don turned to Angela and said:

'Fantastic. Wait till I tell the rest of the team about this. It should mean loads of overtime at least till Christmas.'

Angela replied:

'Don't you believe it, Don. I reckon we'll be looking for new jobs long before then.'

What had Angela heard that Don hadn't? How had two people listening to the same briefing come away with such different impressions?

Many people use only part of their listening ability. Some, Like Don, only **hear** the 'surface' of what is being said. They don't notice the hidden messages that lie beneath the surface. Others, like Angela, really know how to **listen**, and so are able to:

- glean much more valuable information;
- become aware of the hidden meanings behind what is being said;
- recognize the unconscious signals being given out;
- encourage people to reveal more than they had intended.

In this session we will look at the way we use our senses to gather information from those around us and how, by learning to listen 'actively' and observe people's behaviour, we can identify and interpret the real messages hidden in what they say.

2 The five senses

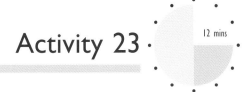

Activity 23 · 12 mins

Go into the reception area of your organization and stand quietly for a few minutes with your eyes shut. Make a mental note of what you hear, smell and feel. When you have finished, write down your observations below.

_____

_____

_____

_____

_____

You will probably have sensed such things as people moving around, the receptionist talking on the telephone or to visitors, a draught coming through the entrance doors, the smell of the furniture, floor polish and perhaps flowers, security cameras.

All this information is being fed into your brain through your five physical senses:

- sight;
- smell;
- hearing;
- taste;
- touch.

They provide you with a huge amount of detail about what is going on around you.

2.1 Perception

The process through which the brain interprets the information received from the senses is called 'perception'.

If, as a first line manager, you can develop your skills of perception, i.e. improve your ability to take in and interpret all the messages received through your five senses, you will be much better able to:

- pick up the hidden meanings in what people say;
- understand how your team members really feel;
- empathize with their problems;
- improve your communication skills;
- read the non-verbal cues which reveal what people really think.

We use our senses to build an image of what the people around us are like and how they will affect us.

But there can be problems. Our interpretation of the information we take in can be distorted by a number of factors that have nothing to do with the information itself. Two of the most significant factors are:

- the environment in which we are receiving the information (for example, whether it is a bright, warm sitting room or a dark, cold, noisy street);
- our memory of similar experiences, places and people we have known in the past.

Activity 24 ·

3 mins

Write down what comes into your mind when you see the words 'Happy New Year'.

_____

_____

_____

The phrase 'Happy New Year' will have triggered in your mind all sorts of sights, sounds and feelings which effect your perception of a happy new year, and which are influenced by your experience of new years in the past.

2.2 Sixth sense

We have another sense, a 'sixth sense', which is independent of our other five senses. Another name for this sense is 'intuition'.

Activity 25 ·

3 mins

What do we mean by 'intuition'? Write down at least three words which you could use to define it.

_____

_____

_____

_____

If you look up 'intuition' in a thesaurus you will find words such as 'impression', 'premonition', 'hunch', 'feeling', 'anticipation' and 'clue'. The dictionary defines it as 'instinctive knowing without the use of rational processes'.

So we could say that intuition is the sense that enables us to 'feel' what people are like, and therefore what they are likely to do and what they are likely to say.

As with the other senses, there are a number of factors which influence our sixth sense and which may interfere with our ability to perceive other people clearly and non-judgementally. They include our:

- background, education and personality;
- experience of similar situations in the past;
- preconceptions of how things **ought** to be;
- self interest, i.e. what suits us best;
- cultural norms, age, gender, class, religion, ethnic origin;
- mind patterns.

2.3 Mind patterns

As a result of the research into neuro-linguistic programming (NLP) in recent years a great deal has become known about the way in which the brain perceives reality. The way each of us perceives that reality is known as our 'mind pattern'. Information is taken into the brain through certain 'filters' and, by learning to manage the filters, you can develop your sixth sense to help you understand and build a rapport with other people.

You use filters to let some information into your mind and keep other information out. For example, you may look at a situation and mainly notice the positive things about it and ignore the negative – one person might think of a foreign holiday in terms of sunlight, relaxation and adventure (positive), while another person only sees airport delays and tummy bugs (negative). They are both seeing the information (the thought of the holiday) through the same filter (the 'Towards/Away from' filter explained below), but each of them is using it in a different way.

Some common types of filter are as follows.

Filter	Characteristic
Towards/Away from	Towards: when thinking about a future goal (such as a wonderful holiday), you tend to imagine what it would be like to achieve it. Away from: when thinking about the future goal, you tend to think about what might stop you achieving it.
Match/Mismatch	 What do you notice about the above shapes? Match: your first thought is that two of the shapes are similar – you always tend to see similarities before differences. Mismatch: your first thought is that one of the shapes is different – you tend to notice differences between things rather than similarities.
Internal/External	Internal: you tend to rely on your own internal feelings to judge whether or not you have done a good job. External: you tend to need external people or events (such as repeat orders) to tell you whether or not you have done a good job.
Past/Present/Future	Past: you like to dwell on the past, and enjoy reminiscing about times gone by. Present: you live for the moment; your attention is on the present. Future: you are constantly planning and thinking about the future.

Activity 26

4 mins

Read the following descriptions and decide which filters each person is using. The first one has been done for you as an example.

1   Eleanor is a great one for living life to the full. She enjoys her job, and knows she is good at it. She plans to be a director by the time she is 30.

Eleanor has 'towards', 'internal' and 'future' filters.

2   Paul loves nothing better than a good argument. He rarely admits that he may be wrong, and can't wait for the day when he will be appointed captain of his local scrabble club.

3   Jan would like to follow in her mother's footsteps and qualify as a librarian. She knows what satisfaction it can bring, but is afraid that she won't be any good at it. The main problem is that she is no good at exams.

The answers to this Activity can be found on page 100.

If the person you are communicating with filters a piece of information in a way which is different from you, then problems of communication are likely to arise.

But once you have recognized the filters that each of you is using, you can choose whether or not to change your filter to match the other person's, so that you are both seeing the situation in the same or complementary ways.

Brian was discussing a change in work rotas with a member of his team, Sally. He thought that if he swapped one of her shifts with Gus, the result would be a much more efficient way of working. But Sally was reluctant. It had been tried before, she said, and hadn't worked and, anyway, they had used the current system for years with no problems.

Sally was filtering the idea of change through the past. To her the past was best. Understanding this, Brian was able to quote instances in the past when such a change had worked well in other teams, and this helped to overcome Sally's reluctance.

3 The communication process

We use spoken communication to send and receive information and messages. This is rarely, if ever, a one-way process. Generally a sender will send a **message** to someone else, whom we call a receiver, and in return is given **feedback**. The message can be distorted by filters (which we have just considered) and interference (which we will look at later in this session).

The communication process therefore looks like this:
The diagram illustrates that communication is an out-and-back process. A

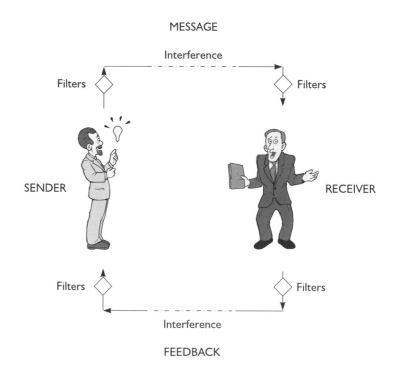

In an effective communication, both sender and receiver need to send messages, and both need to listen.

sender sends a communication out to a receiver, who in turn sends one back. This return communication – feedback – tells the original sender whether or not:

- the message has got through;
- action has been or will be taken;
- the purpose has been achieved.

In other words, feedback tells us whether or not the communication process has worked.

3.1 The importance of feedback

David sits in an enclosed office and keeps the door shut. He can't see or hear the other team members, and they can't see or hear him. When he wants to speak to them, he uses a microphone connected to a loudspeaker outside his office.

There is no doubt that everyone can hear him. The question is: how does David know whether anything is happening as a result?

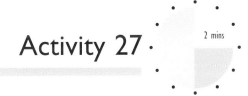

Activity 27   2 mins

Let's imagine that the walls of David's office suddenly vanish, and he makes the same communication face-to-face with his team.

Now how does he know whether anything is happening as a result?

The answer is something that we all experience every day. As David begins to speak:

- the team members first show that they are reacting by paying attention, usually by pausing in their work and turning to look at him;
- they show signs of understanding his message by nodding, making notes or other visual signals;

- they may demonstrate attention by seeking clarification – by asking questions;
- they may signal acceptance of the message by nodding, or saying 'OK', etc.

David will therefore know whether his briefing has been successful by the team members:

- verbally confirming that they have heard and understood;
- demonstrating their understanding in some other way.

3.2 The effect of interference

Research has shown that verbal communication can be very unreliable. It can be affected by blurring, distortion and misinterpretation, and as much as a third can be lost in transmission.

But why do we find it so difficult to listen properly? We're always complaining that other people didn't understand what we meant, or didn't remember what we told them. Yet most of us are just as bad when we listen to others.

On the whole, human beings are rather bad listeners. We fail in three main ways:

> The key issue when you are trying to take in information is to think about the sender.

- we don't concentrate hard enough when we listen;
- we don't always check when we don't understand;
- we find it hard to take in and remember more than a small amount of information at a time.

Activity 28 · 15 mins

Listen to the main news bulletin on the radio or television for 10 minutes. Then make a list of all the news items that were mentioned, in the order in which they were presented.

_____

_____

_____

_____

_____

You may have found it surprisingly difficult to do this Activity. Many people are unable to concentrate totally for 10 minutes. It is something you should keep in mind when briefing your team and others at work.

3.3 Creating barriers

We have already learned that the way we take information in can be distorted by the way we **unconsciously** perceive things.

Listeners may also **consciously** erect barriers against incoming communications, for example, when they:

Becoming a better listener will help you spot problems early, defuse conflicts and maintain effective and productive working relationships.

- don't like the message;
- dislike or mistrust the sender;
- are not motivated to listen;
- think they already know the message;
- have a better idea;
- have something better to say;
- pre-judge the content to be irrelevant, uninteresting, too simple or too complex.

This is quite a serious weakness but something can be done about it:

- speakers can learn to 'package' their communications better;
- listeners can learn to listen better.

4 Learning to listen actively

EXTENSION 2
How to be Twice as Smart is full of useful tips on how to develop your potential as an individual and as a team leader.

In his book *How to be Twice as Smart*, Scott Witt suggests four basic rules for gathering information that other people miss. These rules are as follows:

- encourage others to talk;
- concentrate on content rather than delivery;
- keep your mind open;
- learn to ignore distractions.

Let's look at each of these in turn.

4.1 Encourage others to talk

You may think that listening is a passive activity – you receive the information being transmitted by the other person and that is the end of it. But this isn't true. Listening is much more dynamic than that.

By learning to listen actively, you can control the direction and flow of the conversation, and the amount of detail that the speaker gives. The secret is to show that you are truly interested.

EXTENSION 3
Written in 1936, *How to Win Friends and Influence People* was one of the first books to introduce popular theories on interpersonal relationships to the general public.

In his celebrated book *How to Win Friends and Influence People*, Dale Carnegie tells of the occasion on which he met an eminent botanist at a dinner party in New York. He spent the evening encouraging his fellow guest to tell him about his research into new plant types and the life cycle of the potato.

At the end of the evening, the botanist delightedly told their host that Carnegie was 'most stimulating' and 'a most interesting conversationalist', even though he had hardly uttered a word.

Carnegie had been an excellent listener. He had used his listening skills to:

- give the botanist every opportunity to speak;
- show genuine interest in what he was saying;
- avoid intruding with own his information, interpretations or concerns.

The result was that the botanist had been made to feel important, interesting and valued, and he, in turn, now saw Carnegie in the same light, even though he had uttered scarcely a word throughout the 'conversation'.

4.2 Concentrate on content rather than delivery

One of the high points in the last few political elections in Europe and the USA has often been a pre-election televised debate between the leaders of the main parties. The candidates usually dread them because they know that **the way** they come across to the voters is far more important than **what** they say.

Politicians and others are trained to use persuasive presentation skills to achieve a goal which may not always be in the best interest of their audience.

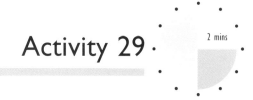

Activity 29

2 mins

Think back to the last time you bought something for yourself that you didn't really want. What made you buy it?

_____

_____

Many people are persuaded to buy products because they have been won over by the charm of the salesperson. Indeed, sales trainees are often taught how to sell **themselves** even more than how to sell the benefits of the **product**.

But if you are aware that you are the subject of such persuasion techniques, you can begin to concentrate on the features of the product itself rather than the salesperson's patter.

4.3 Keep your mind open

If you are listening to someone, but are mentally arguing with what they are saying, you could be blocking out information which, in fact, could be useful to you. You might interrupt him, so that he stops talking, or you might even be tempted to think 'he is talking rubbish', and stop listening altogether.

In either case, you are denying yourself the opportunity of hearing something which could be of some use to you if you listen to it with an open mind.

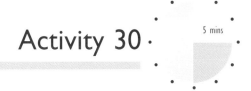

Activity 30

5 mins

Next time you hear someone on television or radio news with whom you usually disagree, instead of mentally 'switching off' listen carefully to what they are saying, and see if you can catch some useful information which you would normally have missed.

4.4 Learn to ignore distractions

Activity 31

4 mins

Imagine that you are attending a presentation on a new piece of technology that will soon be introduced in your work area. Because of accommodation problems the presentation is taking place in the staff restaurant. As it happens, a cleaner is sweeping the floor, three people are eating sandwiches at the next table, and the kitchen staff are noisily preparing lunch in the kitchen next door.

What techniques could you use to help you concentrate on what is being said?

_____

_____

_____

You may have suggested moving closer to the speaker, cupping your hands round your ears, or even asking the speaker to speak up. But there are other techniques which will also help you to ignore such distractions. These are:

■ taking notes;
■ playing mind games;
■ using memory techniques.

Taking notes

In order to take notes of what is being said, you need to take the information in, process it in your mind, and then reproduce it in your own words before writing it down. You can't do this without really concentrating.

Playing mind games

Research has shown that, by playing mental games with what is being said, you can become so involved that there is no room left in your mind for the distraction. You could, for instance, try to pick out the longest word in each sentence or, at regular intervals, make a mental summary of what the speaker is saying.

Using memory techniques

The third technique for avoiding distractions is to use word associations to remember key points in the briefing. This is how it works.

Say, for example, that the speaker is talking about the five characteristics of a good learning objective, i.e. it must be:

Specific;
Measurable;
Achievable;
Relevant;
Time bound.

You would do the following.

1   Think of an acronym that represents the key points – in our example it would be the first letters of each characteristic, i.e. SMART.

2   Now use your imagination to create a scene that links 'SMART' with 'learning objectives'. The more ludicrous the scene the better. So you could, perhaps, visualise a small schoolboy with a huge forehead standing in front of a chalkboard which has the word 'SMART' and 'LEARNING OBJECTIVES' written on it in big red letters.

From now on, when you think of 'learning objectives', your mind will immediately associate it with your imagined scene and the word 'SMART'.

This technique will only work if:

■   you fully understand the facts that you want to remember;
■   you have decided that you really want to remember them.

5 Whole body listening

We have already met some of the ideas involved in the study of neuro-linguistic programming (NLP). Another of its theories is that, if you listen to people with your 'whole body', you will not only hear clearly what they are saying, but you will also gain an insight into what they are thinking and feeling.

To listen to someone in this way, you need to give your total attention – your 'whole body' – to what they are saying and how they are saying it.

EXTENSION 4
Sue Knight's book has many helpful hints on how to use NLP to build successful relationships at work.

According to Sue Knight in her excellent introductory book on NLP, *NLP at Work*, the key to whole body listening is to keep your attention external to yourself rather than being involved in your own thoughts. She compares people whose attention is internal with people who are listening with their whole body.

People whose attention is internal	People who are listening with their whole body
They think their own thoughts, make evaluations and judgements. They worry and concentrate on what just happened, what was just said or even what might happen next.	They are in a state of curiosity. Their attention is entirely on the other person.
Their intention is towards themselves.	Their intention is towards the other person.
Their gaze may be de-focused or moving around.	Their gaze is on the other person.
Their posture could be anything.	They match the other person's posture.
Their language is likely to be 'I', 'me' centred.	Their language is 'you' centred and they use the key words and language patterns that match the person with whom they are speaking.

Activity 32

25 mins

Ask a friend, colleague or family member to help you to carry out this Activity.

Find a quiet location where you won't be interrupted.

1 Talk to your friend for five minutes about any topic you choose. Your friend shouldn't make any interruptions during this time. After five minutes ask him or her to summarise what you said, and what your thoughts and feelings were during the talk. Make a note of any significant misinterpretations, omissions or errors in their summary.

2 Repeat the exercise, but this time ask your friend to talk for five minutes on any topic of their choice. Listen using the whole body listening technique. Then repeat back what you have heard and ask them to comment on the accuracy of your account. Make a note of their comments.

You will probably find that listening with your whole body has enabled you to gather much more information and a much clearer insight into the other person's thoughts and feelings.

6 Hidden messages

There is a Chinese proverb which says:

'A man without a smiling face must not open a shop'.

We are all brought up from a very early age to show an acceptable face to the outside world, whatever we may feel inside. But you only have to watch celebrities and people used to being in the public eye to realize that, very often, what they say is not necessarily what they think or feel.

Activity 33

8 mins

During the next few days make a note of examples of people in the news who are probably not saying what they are really thinking or feeling.

Nearly everything we say has at least two meanings:

- the obvious (overt) meaning, which is open and easily observable;
- the hidden (covert) meanings (which can only be observed through developing your skills of perception).

For example, if a friend tells you that he doesn't want a lift home in your car because it is too far out of your way he could actually be thinking that you are a terrible driver.

By learning to look behind the diplomacy to the hidden meanings in people's speech you can gain great advantages in negotiating with your team and with others around you.

6.1 Flag words

According to Witt, there are certain words ('flag' words) that, when used in conversation, are a pretty reliable sign that the speaker does not mean what he or she is saying. The words are as follows:

EXTENSION 2
See *How to be Twice as Smart* by Scott Witt.

- 'of course', 'naturally', 'no doubt' – used when the speaker thinks that something is highly unlikely. For example, 'Naturally we will consider giving you a rise in six months' time';
- 'by the way', 'incidentally' – used when the speaker wants to make something seem less important than it is. For example, 'By the way, there is a railway line just over the garden wall, but we hardly ever hear anything';
- 'I can't because. . .' – used when someone actually **can**. For example, 'I can't set the deadline any later because my boss won't let me'.

6.2 Content Analysis

Content analysis is a technique used by governments and organizations to decode what other governments and organizations really mean, i.e. what their covert meanings are.

By looking at the frequency with which speakers use certain words or mention certain themes, you can discover what is really on their minds. If one of your team often mentions the benefits of working flexi-hours, it is a good bet that, sooner or later, they will ask for a transfer to a team that offers it.

At this point you should be able to understand how, in the case study at the beginning of this session (see page 37), Content analysis enabled Angela to pick up the hidden messages in the CEO's speech. Even though his overt message was that business was looking up, his mention of recovering market share, discontinued product lines and workforce being below strength all indicated that things were in fact far from well. On their own, none of these things should ring alarm bells but, taken together, they could indicate that something was seriously wrong.

7 Non-verbal communication

When talking to other people, we communicate not only with words but with a whole range of gestures, movements and expressions.

In verbal communication, less than half the message is transmitted through what you say. The rest is transmitted in non-verbal ways.

In this section we will look at ways in which you can pick up both overt and covert messages by observing people's body language.

7.1 Common signs and signals

Before human beings discovered how to talk, and long before they discovered how to write, they communicated – like other animals do – by means of a visual language of physical signals and signs.

Two common signals that we still use in the UK today are:

■ nodding the head to show agreement;
■ giving the 'thumbs up' to show approval.

Activity 34

4 mins

List six or seven other signals that we commonly use to communicate non-verbally.

_____

_____

_____

_____

_____

_____

Suggested answers to this Activity can be found on page 100.

These are large gestures which we use deliberately as an extension of our ordinary language, or in situations where our voices wouldn't be heard, but body language goes much further than this.

7.2 Picking up non-verbal signals

Research has shown that, when communicating, most of us have a natural tendency to make assumptions about the ability of others to 'get the message'. It may simply be because we are lazy, but the danger is that we will overestimate the degree to which they have understood what we are trying to say.

But how can we check that they are keeping up with us?

Activity 35

2 mins

Suppose you have to give complicated instructions to someone about whom you know virtually nothing. How can you judge the level of their knowledge and language ability?

_____

_____

_____

With people you have met before, experience should tell you how much they already know. With people you don't know, the simplest way is to ask them. Ask before you start and ask again as you go along – and you should check their understanding frequently if there is any doubt.

You can also use your eyes, because people unconsciously send out signals and signs all the time. The way they behave will give you a clue as to what is happening in their minds.

Whether you are speaking to one person or a group, the unconscious body language of your listeners gives you enormously valuable feedback. You will be able to tell whether or not you are holding their attention, and whether or not you are getting your messages across.

Activity 36

2 mins

Suppose you are telling work-experience trainees about the work your section does. What visual signs would show that you are not holding their attention?

_____

_____

_____

Humans are usually much better at recognizing body language than at listening to speech – it's a skill our species acquired much, much earlier.

There are many signs that you should recognize. We have all sent similar signals in our time.

Signs of boredom:

■ saying 'uh huh', 'yes', or 'right' before you have finished a sentence;
■ looking around.

Meaning: they want you to get on with it.

Signs of difficulty keeping up:

■ puzzled expression (furrowed brow, screwed-up eyes, etc.);
■ scratched heads.

Meaning: they are still trying, but they have trouble keeping up with you.

Signs of failing concentration:

■ yawning, looking at their watches, looking around;
■ doodling, fidgeting, picking, scratching, shuffling, passing notes.

Meaning: you are losing them fast – they have stopped trying to concentrate.

EXTENSION 5
A helpful book on the subject of body language is _Body Talk: The Skills of Positive Image_ by Judi James.

Signs of having given up:

■ glazed expressions;
■ falling asleep.

Meaning: you've lost them – and you probably won't be able to get them back.

7.3 Responding to conflicting messages

Body language sends messages. When these are consistent with the verbal messages we're trying to communicate there is no problem – the body language reinforces the verbal message.

But when the body language is telling a different story from the verbal message the credibility of the message is weakened. The simplest example of this is when someone tries to make a genuine and sincere statement but is unable make eye contact with the audience.

We use a wide range of facial expressions and body movements that reveal our feelings and our reactions to other people. Often we use these signs without consciously intending to, and often they don't reflect what we are saying.

So how should you react if somebody's body language sends a message which is different from their speech?

We all learn to recognize these signs. We can tell by people's behaviour whether they are excited, bored, tired, mystified, irritated, friendly, hostile, nervous or angry.

Even if you are talking to someone on the telephone, where you can't see each other's body language, you can still hear subtle hesitations and changes in tone which reveal the other person's true feelings.

If you recognize such signs, you have to decide whether you are going to believe:

- their words, or
- their body language.

> Frank was briefing some colleagues on his section's re-organization plans. One or two of them looked interested, nodded from time to time and took notes. However, Frank noticed a couple of others who seemed to spend most of the time doodling, gazing at the posters on the office wall and fiddling with their fingernails.
>
> When he'd finished, Frank looked all round the group and asked 'Does anyone have any questions?' One of the people who had been taking notes asked a question, but neither of the 'doodlers' did. Frank made a final attempt to check: 'Is everyone happy?' All those present either nodded agreement or murmured 'Yes'. But sure enough, it later turned out that the doodlers hadn't grasped the main point of the briefing at all. A couple of weeks later Frank had to brief them all over again.

Activity 37

2 mins

In this case study Frank was right about what the doodlers' body language was telling him. What could he have done in the circumstances?

_____

_____

_____

If Frank had been a school teacher, he would probably have put the doodlers on the spot by asking them some searching questions. However, you just can't do that with colleagues.

The alternative would be to make an extra effort to engage their interest, perhaps by:

■ making more eye contact with them than with the others present;
■ making references to how their particular departments or functions might be affected by his plans;
■ inviting them to contribute to the discussion.

In any situation where a person's body language and words conflict, your best approach is to try to break down any barriers between you and build a good rapport.

We will look at rapport in Session C.

Self-assessment 2

15 mins

1   We use our _____ to build an image of what the people around us are like and how they will effect us.

2   What are our five physical senses?

_____

_____

3   The communication process consists of a sender sending a _____ to a receiver, and in return receiving _____.

4   Why is feedback so important in the communication process?

_____

_____

5   Suggest three techniques which will help you to ignore distractions when someone is speaking.

_____

_____

_____

6   What is the secret of active listening?

_____

_____

_____

7   The following list contains descriptions of (1) people whose attention is internal and (2) people who listen with their whole body. Tick the boxes to indicate which is which.

Type of listener	Their attention is internal	They are listening with their whole body
They think their own thoughts, make evaluations and judgements. They worry and concentrate on what just happened, what was just said or even what might happen next.		
Their gaze is on the other person.		
They are in a state of curiosity. Their attention is entirely on the other person.		
Their language is likely to be 'I', 'me' centred.		

8   Suggest two ways in which you can judge the level of knowledge and language ability of someone about whom you know virtually nothing.

9   How might a speaker's body language:

a reduce the speaker's credibility?

b weaken the speaker's message?

Answers to these questions can be found on pages 98–9.

8 Summary

- Human beings are bad listeners because:

  - we don't concentrate hard enough when we listen;
  - we don't always check when we don't understand;
  - we find it hard to take in and remember more than a small amount of information at a time;
  - we erect barriers against people and things that we misjudge, misunderstand or simply don't want to hear.

- Good listeners are able to:

  - glean much more valuable information;
  - become aware of the hidden meanings behind what is being said;
  - recognize the unconscious signals being given out;
  - encourage people to reveal more than they had intended.

- We have five physical senses, sight, smell, hearing, taste and touch.

- The sixth sense is intuition.

- We use filters to let certain information into our minds and keep other information out.

- Feedback tells us whether or not the communication process has been successful.

- Up to 30% of verbal communication can be lost in transmission.

- We can gather more information by:

  - encouraging others to talk;
  - concentrating on content rather than delivery;
  - keeping our minds open;
  - learning to ignore distractions.

- Whole body listening involves keeping our attention focused outside ourselves.

- In verbal communication, less than half the message is transmitted through what we say. The rest is transmitted in non-verbal ways.

- In any situation where a person's body language and words conflict, the best approach is to try to break down barriers and build a good rapport.

Session C
Building a network

1 Introduction

Consider Robert. . .

Robert was an only child. When he was a boy, most Sunday afternoons had been spent on railway platforms, sharing his father's passion for train spotting. At school he had worked hard, preferring to stay behind in the computer room when his classmates played five-a-side football in the playground. He did well in his exams, and won a place to study computer science at university. He made few friends during his student years; he saw no point in spending money in pubs, and believed that the most important thing in life was to justify his parents' belief in him by getting a good degree. This he did.

On graduating, Robert got a job as an IT support technician in an international company not far from his home. His parents were delighted as this meant that he could move back into his old bedroom.

A year later the company hit hard times and Robert was made redundant. There were no jobs around for support technicians, and Robert had no idea what else he could do. The future looked bleak.

Ziggy, on the other hand, had always loved people around her. Her first memory was playing Mary in the school nativity play. She had adored Brownies, learned to ice skate with a crowd of friends, and had been head of nearly every sports team in her school. When she did her Duke of Edinburgh Award, she became deeply involved in supporting underprivileged families in her area and raising money for them. Everyone missed her when she went off to college to do media studies.

College life was fast and furious. Ziggy became a leading light of the drama, square dance and mountaineering clubs, and helped organize numerous social events, culminating in the graduation ball at the end of her final year. When she got a job on one of the national newspapers, no one was a bit surprised.

But, like Robert, Ziggy was made redundant. The paper was taken over and her job was no longer needed. As soon as she heard, Ziggy began firing off emails to everyone she could think of, and within two weeks an old university friend had put her in touch with an international charity which, impressed with her history of social work, hired her to join their international marketing team.

Activity 38

3 mins

What did Ziggy have going for her in her working life that Robert didn't?

_____

_____

Ziggy was very much a 'people' person. She liked nearly everyone she met, understood how to build relationships, and knew how to use those relationships to further her job prospects. In contrast Robert was thoroughly introvert. He looked to things rather than people for his emotional support, and when he was in trouble he didn't have the contacts or social skills to help him get back on his feet.

This session looks at why Ziggy was so much more successful than Robert in relating to people. You will learn how her skill at networking can be developed and maintained in the workplace, and how everyone – you, your team and the organization – can benefit from close-knit, effective networking relationships.

2 What is networking?

2.1 A definition

Networking can be defined as:

'the creation and use of personal contacts for one's own benefit or for the benefit of a group'.

In other words, a network is a set of contacts you develop to promote your career or some other interest.

Networking can be used in any context: at work, in your social life or any other situation. The point is that you are using your contacts with other people to help yourself and them to become more successful.

Ziggy had built up a large network of friends and contacts during her time at school and university, and she was able to use these to further her career when the job market got tough.

2.2 How does a network differ from any other social group?

You are probably already a member of one or more groups of friends or acquaintances who spend time together.

Activity 39 ·

Think about the contacts you have (1) at work and (2) socially with whom you have a friendly relationship. Write some of their names below.

Work contacts

_____

_____

_____

_____

_____

Social contacts

_____

_____

_____

_____

_____

You will probably be surprised at how many names you wrote down of people with whom you have some kind of relationship.

A network is different from a group of friends because its sole purpose is to develop a means of interaction which will benefit either you alone or all its members generally. It provides a reservoir of people who have specialist knowledge and contacts that will help you to achieve your chosen objectives.

So it is a much more structured organism than a group of friends and colleagues.

Activity 40

4 mins

Look at the names that you wrote down in the last Activity. Now carry out the same exercise again, but this time limit the names to those people whose knowledge you can use to develop some enterprise or interest you have.

Work contacts

_____

_____

_____

_____

Social contacts

_____

_____

_____

_____

You should now be able to appreciate the difference between a group of friends or colleagues and a network; the former is not necessarily useful to you in achieving your objectives whereas the latter is.

3 What's good about networking?

EXTENSION 2
In his book _How to be Twice as Smart_ Scott Witt describes the benefits of networking.

Networking lets you:

- tap into the knowledge and experience of other people, without having to learn or experience those things yourself;
- access the latest information as and when you need it;
- help other people by offering your own knowledge and experience;
- become an expert in areas which may not be covered adequately in reference materials;

- understand a topic from the point of view of people who have practical experience of it, not just the theory;
- build loyalty and rapport with a group of people who can help each other to achieve their individual aims.

4 Types of network

Networks can be classified in various ways. We will look at two types of classification:

- internal networks/external networks;
- knowledge networks/self-interest groups.

4.1 Internal and external networks

Networks relating to your work can be either internal to the organization or external.

Internal networks

Your internal network is likely to consist of colleagues in your own department and in other areas of your organization.

By building links with such people you can obtain information that enables you to:

If you find out what opposition you are likely to meet before it happens, you can take preventative action.

- build a good team;
- give and receive support from other team leaders;
- learn new skills;
- identify areas for development;
- access knowledge and experience held by specialists in other work areas;
- promote changes which you would like to introduce in your work area;
- lobby the people whose support you need to achieve your objectives;
- find out about potential opposition to your plans.

Internal networks are built naturally through your everyday working activities, but if they are to be really effective you have to spend time developing and nurturing them.

You could, for instance:

■ establish regular email correspondence with someone in another section who might have information or contacts that could help you in the future;

■ join committees relating to your work, union or a company social club;

■ become a member of a company sports team.

Every contact made through these actions could prove helpful to you in achieving your personal or work objectives at some time in the future.

External networks

External networks are those you develop with people outside your organization, such as former colleagues or people working for other companies in the same industry. Networks outside the organisation can be helpful in many ways:

■ if your job is threatened, external contacts in the same line of business might know of other vacancies elsewhere;

■ talking to other people can help you to gain information, identify training courses, find useful web sites, and so on, all of which could help you develop your career.

Strategies for developing external networks include:

■ joining special interest clubs which have relevance to your work (such as the student organizations which exist under the umbrella of some professions);

■ using Internet chat rooms relating to particular subject areas;

■ developing social links with people from other organizations in your industry.

You can also use external networks to help you in the social side of your life, for instance to:

■ make new friends when you move to a new neighbourhood;

■ find out the best schools, doctors, dentists, shops;

■ locate reliable experts such as plumbers and electricians;

■ find out about local organizations such as sports clubs, yoga classes or pub music nights.

4.2 Knowledge networks and mutual interest networks

Another way of classifying networks is to divide them into:

■ those that you use specifically to promote your own interests, for example, to develop your career or gain a new skill (known as knowledge networks);

■ those whose aim is to benefit all members equally (mutual interest networks).

Knowledge networks

No one can know everything they need to know all the time – for one thing it would soon be out of date. A much more efficient solution is to be able to contact the person who **does** have the latest information, at the time when you need it.

A knowledge network is a ready-reference list of people who are willing and able to give you the information you need when you need it. By creating a knowledge network you can:

- find out the best way to develop your career;
- avoid making mistakes;
- obtain all the information you need to make major decisions;
- build up background data on a situation before you get involved in it.

Steve wanted to buy a new home computer. He already used computers for simple spreadsheet tasks at work, but didn't really understand all the terminology. The magazine adverts looked impressive, but he really had no idea of the best specification for his particular needs: helping his daughter with her homework and working through his home study course on computing. What Steve needed was a knowledge network.

He needed to find people who could tell him about different computer specifications, the advantages and disadvantages of each, and what the best specification would be for him. Any computer shop would have a vested interest in the advice it gave him; he would be much wiser to talk to an experienced colleague or members of the local computer club.

The important thing about knowledge networks is that you should never include anyone who is involved financially in that particular subject area or interest. Only ask for information or advice from people who have nothing to lose by giving it to you. So, for instance, you should never ask:

- an accountant for free advice on your tax return;
- a surveyor to look at your house subsidence as a favour;
- a solicitor to comment on the advice you have received from another law firm.

But you **could** ask any of them for advice on anything else about which they have expert knowledge – so long as it isn't something for which they usually charge.

You might well ask why such people should be prepared to give you information in the first place. What are they going to get out of it?

Well, we have already seen in Session B that people like to be made to feel valued and important – and most people are naturally helpful anyway. So long as they don't feel that they are being exploited, the vast majority of people are only too keen to offer help and advice on their pet subject if they are asked in the right way.

Mutual interest networks

Certain types of knowledge are best learned by joining a group of people who all share their knowledge with each other. Examples include computer groups, share investment groups and groups which form to develop a particular hobby, such as antiques or travel.

Mutual interest networks (MINs) are different from clubs because there is no formal structure – no official membership, no secretary and no committee. They are just a group of people who enjoy sharing their knowledge and enthusiasm for a particular topic. Every member of the network benefits because every member shares information and supports the others.

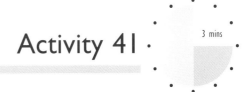

Activity 41

3 mins

Think about your own interests, both inside your organization and outside. Are there any areas in which you would find it useful to form a MIN?

5 Creating a network

Victoria had worked at the bank for five years. She had passed all her banking exams with flying colours but had hit a 'glass ceiling' – no matter how hard she tried, she just couldn't get promotion within her section of the bank.

Then she read a self-help book on 'How to network effectively', and decided to try out its theories. We will follow her progress during the rest of this section.

Victoria's self-help book explained that developing a network involves the following steps:

1 decide **why** you want to network;

2 decide on a strategy;

3 carry out research;

4 develop the network.

5.1 Decide why you want to network

EXTENSION 6
See *Networking for Success* by Carol Harris for more advice on developing a network.

There are any number of reasons why you might need to obtain knowledge through networking. You might, for example, want to:

■ learn more about a new piece of technology you would like to introduce at work;
■ research the potential for a career move;
■ develop your interest in a particular hobby.

In Victoria's case the purpose was clear: she wanted to develop a network that would help her to advance her career in banking.

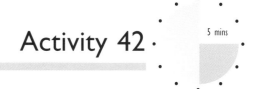

Activity 42 · 5 mins

S/NVQ D1.1

This Activity, together with Activities 43, 44 and 45 may provide the basis of appropriate evidence for your S/NVQ portfolio. If you are intending to take this course of action, it might be better to write your answers on separate sheets of paper.

Choose a project to do with either your work or leisure activities in which obtaining expert knowledge from other people could be useful e.g. you might ask a professional caterer about how much food you should serve at a buffet for 180 people. Briefly describe the project and the knowledge you would like to obtain.

_____

_____

_____

5.2 Decide on a strategy

SWOT analysis is usually used in an organizational context. However, it can also be used to assess individuals.

You need to think about the strategy you will use to get the knowledge. It is useful to start with a SWOT analysis which involves analysing your:

- **S**trengths;
- **W**eaknesses;
- **O**pportunities;
- **T**hreats.

You might find that, in developing a network:

- strengths could include the people you know already or any particular ally you already have whom you might call on for help;
- weaknesses could include such things as lack of time or poor communication skills;
- opportunities could include clubs you might join or having access to the Internet;
- threats could include other people resenting your networking activities or opposing the reason for your networking (such as getting a better job).

As far as Victoria was concerned she felt that her main strengths were her friendly personality and the fact that she already worked in a bank. Her main weakness was that being a woman made it more difficult to get promotion in the bank. Her opportunities included the fact that there were other women in the bank who could help her, and she knew that one of the few female senior managers played for the bank's badminton team. Victoria was very good at badminton. Her only threat was that she didn't get on with her immediate manager, so might get some opposition from him.

Activity 43

10 mins

S/NVQ D1.1

This Activity, together with Activities 42, 44 and 45 may provide the basis of appropriate evidence for your S/NVQ portfolio. If you are intending to take this course of action, it might be better to write your answers on separate sheets of paper.

Think about the strengths, weaknesses, opportunities and threats relating to your own project. Make a list of them.

Strengths

_____

_____

Weaknesses

_____

_____

Opportunities

_____

_____

Threats

_____

_____

You may have had a number of ideas. The list will probably grow as you get further into your planning.

Once you have done a SWOT analysis, you can develop a detailed strategy for building your network.

You might, for example, decide that one of your strengths is access to a number of clubs or societies where you can find helpful people, while a weakness is that you are not very good at using your interpersonal skills. So part of your strategy might be to do an open learning course on rapport building. You will learn more about building rapport later in this section.

Other strategies might include:

- making lists of everyone you know already who might be useful to you;
- getting your line manager to support you;
- joining appropriate clubs;
- getting access to the Internet;
- watching what other people around you do to build effective networks;
- finding ways to incorporate your networking activities into your everyday life.

Victoria decided that her main strategies would be to:

- join the bank's badminton team;
- develop a network of the women in her bank and in other banks in the town.

By taking these steps she would gain:

- advance information of any vacancies that cropped up in any local bank;
- a way of getting to know the female senior manager in her own bank;
- information on how other women had dealt with a glass ceiling in the past.

Activity 44 · 10 mins

S/NVQ D1.1

This Activity, together with Activities 42, 43 and 45 may provide the basis of appropriate evidence for your S/NVQ portfolio. If you are intending to take this course of action, it might be better to write your answers on separate sheets of paper.

Make a list of the strategies you will use to develop your network.

_____

_____

_____

_____

5.3 Carry out research

In the last step we saw how, in deciding on a strategy, you should make a list of all those contacts you have already who have knowledge that could be useful to you. (This was the 'strengths' part of the SWOT analysis.) The list might be quite short, but it is just the start.

Each person on it will be able to put you in touch with other people who also have useful knowledge, and in the research phase you should follow up those leads by contacting the people concerned.

The research stage also involves identifying the clubs, social groups, computer chat rooms and other groupings where you might meet the people who can help you. You could do this by:

- viewing appropriate web sites;
- looking at trade magazines;
- consulting lists of clubs, societies and trade associations in the local library;

- asking company switchboards for contact details of appropriate members of staff in your own and other organizations;
- checking courses offered by the local further education college;
- contacting relevant professional bodies.

Victoria decided that a good place to start her research would be her local association of the Institute of Financial Services (ifs). She visited the ifs website and discovered:

- the contact details of her local ifs association and a programme of their meetings;
- an annual series of Financial Innovations Awards, one of whose categories was for the best customer relationship management strategy;
- an annual Awards dinner where she would be able to meet useful people;
- a careers development section containing a course aimed at a BSc (Hons) in Financial Services and Associateship;
- a career development service;
- a student learning support (SLS) team.

She decided to find out more about all of these.

Activity 45

S/NVQ D1.1

This Activity, together with Activities 42, 43 and 44 may provide the basis of appropriate evidence for your S/NVQ portfolio. If you are intending to take this course of action, it might be better to write your answers on separate sheets of paper.

Make your own list of contacts and social groups that could be useful to you in your own networking project.

5.4 Develop your network

You have chosen the people to contact, clubs to join and projects to get involved in – all that's left now is to actually start networking.

You don't have to be brazen-faced by asking your contacts directly for the information you want. There is a huge amount that you can glean from a casual conversation which has been steered round to the general topic area.

But what do you do if you have been given the name of someone you have never met before? How can you approach them?

There are three particularly useful techniques:

- mention the name of the person who referred you – for example: 'Anne Davies suggested that you might be able to advise me on . . .';
- make the person feel important – for example, 'I have been told that you know everything there is to know about . . .';
- make a straightforward appeal for help – for example, 'I would be really grateful if you would tell me how to . . .'.

But remember, never ask for free information from an expert whose business involves providing it for a fee.

6 Building rapport

6.1 We all need to relate

Your success at networking will depend on your ability to build effective relationships.

Activity 46

35 mins

Next time you are in a social environment such as the staff restaurant, the pub, at home with the family, or somewhere else where you normally meet people socially, try an experiment.

For the first 15 minutes avoid communicating with anyone – no talking, no smiling, no eye contact. During the next 15 minutes look happy, chat with people you meet, crack a joke or two (if you are good at it), and show real interest in everything that is going on around you.

Look at the words below and underline all those words which you think would reflect your feelings at the end if the first 15 minutes; then circle all the words which would reflect your feelings at the end of the second 15 minutes.

happy	shy	embarrassed	self-aware
depressed	optimistic	bored	warm
frustrated	anxious	kind	confident
respected	enthusiastic	ill at ease	tired
successful	disliked	inferior	excluded
funny	sociable	depressed	stimulating
liked	nervous	boring	resentful

The odds are that you underlined most of the negative words to describe the first 15 minutes, and positive ones for the second period when you were chatting to people and communicating generally.

Communication is essential if we are to feel comfortable in the society of other people. And networking is all about communicating well.

Effective communication is based on rapport, i.e. the ability to see the other person's point of view. If you have rapport with someone you are 'on the same wavelength' – even though you don't necessarily share the same opinions. You feel easy in their company, conversation is relaxed and silences are not awkward. You often intuitively know what the other person is thinking, and can understand and empathize with their feelings.

People who share rapport show it in many physical ways. They:

- mirror each other's actions and posture;
- laugh at the same time;
- move in the same rhythm;
- look in the same direction.

They will often do this quite unconsciously, and may often be able to divine each other's thoughts and feelings.

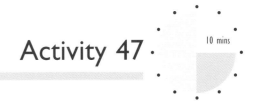

Activity 47

Observe the people you are working with during the next couple of days. Do any of them show signs of rapport? If so, what are those signs?

_____

_____

_____

Most of the indicators of rapport consist of matching **physical** behaviour – posture, movement, voice tones and so on. But the rapport between two people will be even stronger if they also share common **values** (such as honesty, truthfulness, loyalty, commitment) and **beliefs** (for example, that everyone is of value or that there is no such thing as failure).

6.2 How to build rapport

If you can build a rapport with someone, you are more likely to be able to network with them than with those you can't.

So how do you build rapport with someone if it doesn't exist naturally between you?

The key is to match their behaviour by:

■ matching the way they stand and the way they hold their body;
■ holding your arms, hands and fingers in the same way;
■ copying the way they hold their head and shoulders;
■ looking in the same direction as they do;
■ following their gaze;
■ breathing at the same rate;
■ breathing from the same part of the body (lungs, abdomen, stomach);
■ walking to the same rhythm;
■ speaking at the same pitch, volume and pace;
■ using the same kinds of words and terminology.

You can also use the lessons we learned about mind patterns in Session A to complement the filters they use in processing information. For example, note whether their filters are towards or away from, past, present or future, match or mismatch, internal or external. Then adopt an approach that complements them.

Activity 48 · 10 mins

During the next few days practise your skills of matching with people you meet. Make a note of their reactions. Does conversation flow more easily? Is the atmosphere more relaxed? Have you been successful in building a rapport with them?

6.3 Some final tips

This session has looked at the steps involved in developing a network from scratch. But the basic principles of networking can be applied at every point in your life, both at work and at home.

Here are a few final tips for your to practise until they become second nature to you:

- remember people's names, and use them frequently when talking to them;
- never leave a meeting or other gathering wishing you had spoken to someone;
- find out about the people you are going to contact; know what their interests and priorities are;
- when you meet new contacts for the first time, don't try to pick their brains there and then; get in touch with them later;
- dress smartly so that people notice and remember you;
- always have your contact details with you – and a pen and paper to write down other people's details;
- always keep your promises. If you have said you will do something, do it;
- always send a thank you note after a party;
- form a bond with someone by asking them to do you a favour;
- whenever possible, give people something – even if it is just some notes or a useful telephone number;
- smile.

Self-assessment 3

15 mins

1 Networking can be defined as the creation and use of personal contacts for one's own _____ or for the _____ of a group.

2 What is the difference between a network and a social group?

_____

_____

3 What are the two ways in which networks can be classified?

_____

_____

4 Suggest three ways in which you could develop an internal network.

_____

_____

_____

5 What kind of network is designed specifically to benefit all members equally.

_____

6 Who should you never ask for advice when you are networking?

_____

7 What does SWOT stand for?

_____

8 Can you have rapport with someone if you don't share their opinions?

_____

Answers to these questions can be found on page 99.

7 Summary

- Networking is the creation and use of personal contacts for one's own benefit or for the benefit of a group.

- Networking can be used in any context.

- A network is different from a group of friends because its sole purpose is to develop a means of interaction which will benefit its members.

- Networking lets every member of the network:

  - tap into the knowledge and experience of other people without having to learn or experience those things themselves;
  - access the latest information as and when they need it;
  - help other people by offering their own knowledge and experience;
  - become an expert in areas which may not be covered adequately in reference materials;
  - understand a topic from the point of view of people who have practical experience of it, not just the theory;
  - build loyalty and rapport with a group of people who can help each other to achieve their individual aims.

- Two classifications of 'networking' are:

  - internal networks/external networks;
  - knowledge networks/mutual interest networks.

- You should only ask for information or advice from people who have nothing to lose by giving it to you.

- To develop a network you must:

  - decide why you want to network;
  - decide on a strategy;
  - carry out research;
  - develop the network.

- One of your first strategies is to make a list of all those contacts you have already who have knowledge that could be useful to you.

- Your success at networking will depend on your ability to build effective relationships.

- Having rapport means that you are on the same wavelength as someone – even if you don't share their opinions.

Performance checks

1 Quick quiz

Question 1   What is the main purpose of a briefing?

_____

_____

Question 2   What three rules should you remember when briefing people you don't know much about?

_____

_____

_____

Question 3   What five steps are involved in planning and preparing a briefing or presentation?

_____

_____

_____

_____

_____

Question 4   Which part of the briefing or presentation should you design first?

_____

Question 5   Before you begin your briefing or presentation, you should check that:

- all your _____ _____ are ready;

- the _____ is set up and working properly.

Question 6 Suggest four techniques for making sure that your message gets across to your audience.

_____

_____

_____

_____

Question 7 What is the process through which the brain interprets information received from the senses?

_____

Question 8 '_____' is the sense that enables us to 'feel' what people are like.

Question 9 Fill in the empty boxes.

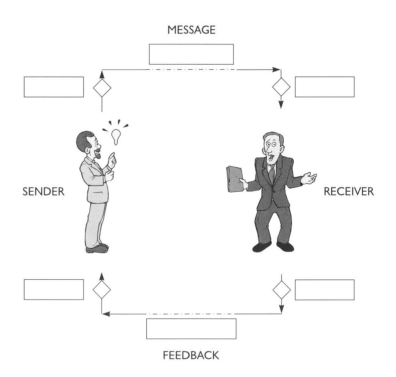

MESSAGE

SENDER

RECEIVER

FEEDBACK

Question 10 What three pieces of information does feedback give the original sender of a message?

_____

_____

_____

Question 11   What are 'of course', 'naturally', 'by the way' and 'I can't because. . .' examples of?

Question 12   What do the letters SWOT stand for?

Question 13   Suggest three strategies you could use in forming an external network.

Question 14   A _____ _____ is a ready-reference list of people who are willing and able to give you the information you need when you need it.

Question 15   A _____ _____ _____ is a group of people who enjoy sharing knowledge and enthusiasm for a particular topic.

Answers to these questions can be found on pages 100–2.

2 Workbook assessment

60 mins

Read the following case incident and then deal with the questions which follow, writing your answers on a separate sheet of paper.

Angelica Kiprianou has just taken over as day-shift first line manager in the technical support department of a large insurance company. The department's role is to solve computer and telecommunications problems for staff in other departments. Since much of the company's business is done by telephone, fax and e-mail, and virtually everyone uses computers, this is a crucial role. The workload is heavy and the pressures are intense.

Angelica's predecessor, Keith Roberts, was a notorious 'hard man' who supervised everyone extremely strictly. His objectives for his team were simple: repair faults quickly, but avoid if at all possible replacing faulty equipment with new. Any complaint about slowness in carrying out a repair made him furious; he was equally angry if a technician decided to replace a unit instead of repairing it. Roberts, who was a big man, would stomp into the repair shop and shout abuse at the culprit in front of the whole department. This aside, though, he was uncommunicative. The team had little idea of what the company as a whole was doing, or of how their own work fitted into the broader picture.

Angelica is quite different – she is a competent first line manager while being pleasant and quietly spoken. She does not want to run the department in the way that Roberts did – and probably couldn't even if she wanted to.

After a few weeks, Angelica notices that costs are increasing and that faulty equipment is piling up. She soon realizes that the technicians are taking advantage of her by replacing equipment with new units instead of repairing the faults. This suits both the customers and the technicians. However, it is very wasteful, and Angelica will in due course be accountable for the rising cost of new equipment.

She also notes that technicians are tending to dump replaced equipment in the store room without any indication of what the fault was. This will cause much confusion and extra work when someone finally sits down to repair these units; and, naturally enough, the backlog of repairs is steadily growing.

Angelica needs to restore the working practices that Roberts had established, but in her own way.

She decides to have a team briefing.

Carry out the following tasks:

1   Make a list of the key points and subsidiary points that Angelica would include in the briefing, then write brief notes for an introduction, summary and conclusion.

2   Suggest what actions she could take before the briefing to discover how the team are likely to react to the restoration of the old working practices.

3   It is rumoured that the manager of the technical support department is due to retire in six months' time. How could Angelica use networking to help her in a bid for his job?

S/NVQ D1.1,
D1.2

3 Work-based assignment

The time guide for this assignment gives you an idea of how long it is likely to take you to write up your findings. You will find that you need to spend some additional time gathering information, perhaps talking to colleagues and thinking about the assignment. The result of your efforts should be presented as speaking notes and draft visual aids, plus a recording on audio or video cassette.

Your written response to this assignment may form useful evidence for your S/NVQ portfolio. The assignment is designed to help you demonstrate your skills in:

- communicating;
- influencing others;
- searching for information.

What you should do

Organize with your manager that you will give a presentation to your team on a topic about which you believe they need to be more aware. This could be on health and safety, data protection and confidentiality, security, new work procedures or a change in the organization's structure.

Prepare a presentation on the topic; it should not take more than 10 minutes in its final form.

Make neat drafts of three flip-chart pages or three OHP slides which you would propose to use as visual aids.

- Prepare a neat copy of the notes from which you would speak.
- Practise and rehearse delivering the presentation, perhaps with the help of friends.
- When you are happy with it, make an audio or video recording of the presentation (depending on what facilities you have available).

Remember that your presentation should cover all the key points while not taking more than 10 minutes to deliver.

Reflect and review

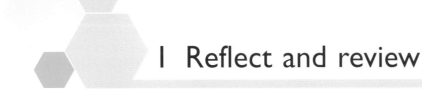

1 Reflect and review

Now that you have completed your work on networking and sharing information let's review the workbook objectives. The first objective was:

■ prepare and deliver effective briefings to your team, and contribute to briefings given by others.

On completion of this workbook you will be better able to ensure that when you give a briefing, your listeners will understand you clearly.

Thinking about the audience is the key to successful briefings, whether it is on a one-to-one basis or in front of a group.

Listeners are all different, and you cannot always assume that they understand the jargon of your workplace or share your understanding of the subject. People misunderstand each other easily enough in ordinary life; at work it pays for managers and team leaders to make certain that their messages are getting through. There are two main points to remember:

■ some listeners may need more explanation than others;
■ you need to check their understanding.

Think about the range of people you have to brief, and the different things you need to say to them.

■ Who needs more explanation?

■ How will you check understanding?

_____

_____

■ How can you improve your presentation skills?

_____

_____

_____

The second workbook objective was:

■ use your senses to gather information from those around you.

Communication is a two-way process: we send messages out and we receive feedback in return. But many messages have hidden (or covert) meanings which we need to be able to pick up. This is done through the five physical senses together with the sixth sense, intuition. But messages can be distorted by mind filters and interference.

Things to think about include:

■ What filters do you and the other members of your team use that might get in the way of clear communication?

_____

_____

_____

■ How can you ensure that the messages you send and receive are not distorted by interference?

_____

_____

_____

■ How can you help your team to communicate more clearly?

_____

_____

_____

The next objective was:

■ use the technique of whole body listening to pick up hidden messages.

Whole body listening enables us to concentrate thoroughly on the messages being communicated to us. We can tell a lot about what someone really means by noting the way they speak, the types of words they use, and their body language.

You could think about the following questions:

■ What are the hidden messages that you receive every day but which, up to now, you have not identified?

_____

_____

_____

■ What hidden messages do you give out when communicating with your team which reduce the impact of what you are trying to say?

_____

_____

_____

■ What steps can you take to develop the skill of whole body listening – for both you and your team?

_____

_____

_____

The last objective was:

■ explain the value of networking, and create a network to promote both your work objectives and social interests.

Networking puts at your disposal a huge reservoir of knowledge and experience which you otherwise would not have. In a knowledge network the people in it are normally unaware of the fact that they are providing information purely in order for you to achieve your set objectives. They are happy to provide information because it makes them feel valued.

Mutual interest networks exist for the benefit of all the members. Everyone contributes knowledge and expertise for the benefit of everyone else in the network.

The success of all networking depends on your skill at building rapport.

Think about:

■ What personal objective do you have which could be helped by developing a knowledge network?

_____

_____

_____

■ What networks do you already have at work which could provide you with useful information?

_____

_____

_____

■ What steps will you take to build rapport with the people around you?

_____

_____

_____

2 Action plan

Use this plan to further develop for yourself a course of action you want to take. Make a note in the left-hand column of the issues or problems you want to tackle, and then decide what you intend to do, and make a note in column 2.

The resources you need might include time, materials, information or money. You may need to negotiate for some of them, but they could be something easily acquired, like half an hour of somebody's time, or a chapter of a book. Put whatever you need in column 3. No plan means anything without a timescale, so put a realistic target completion date in column 4.

Finally, describe the outcome you want to achieve as a result of this plan, whether it is for your own benefit or advancement, or a more efficient way of doing things.

Desired outcomes	1 Issues	2 Action	3 Resources	4 Target completion

Actual outcomes

3 Extensions

Extension 1

Using visual aids

The **overhead projector** (OHP) is one of the simplest and most effective visual aids. It is particularly valuable for keeping important points in front of your listeners while you are talking about them. OHPs are useful for diagrams, cartoons and other illustrations, as well as text.

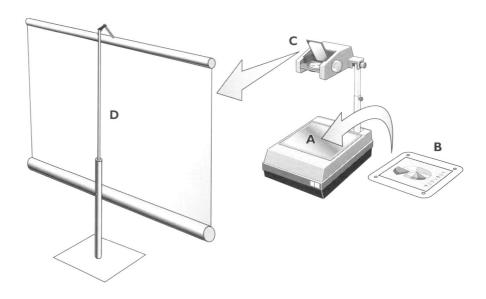

It is basically a box with a back-lit opaque panel on the top (A). You place your slide (B) on top of this panel, and the lens (C) picks up the image and casts it onto a screen (D). This creates a greatly enlarged image, big enough for the audience to read.

Making OHP slides is very easy. The slides themselves are made of heat-resistant plastic film, and all you need to write on them is one or two special felt-tip pens in different colours. The techniques for successful OHP slides are:

OHP slides can also be prepared on a computer and printed out through a laser or ink-jet printer. You can add colour by hand if necessary.

- write or draw clearly;
- write or draw neatly;
- don't try to cram on too much information.

In fact it is most important to draft out your OHP sheet on plain paper, to make sure you have got it right before you put pen to plastic!

Here are two examples of OHP slides, both much reduced from the normal size of about 20 cm × 30 cm:

Bad *Good*

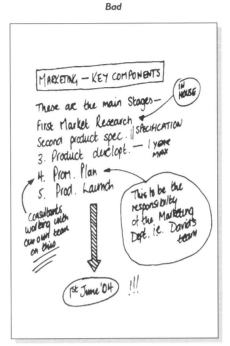
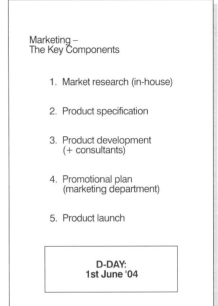

When you are talking about what the slide shows, you can point to particular parts of it, and there are techniques for this too:

■ use a pencil or a pointer and point to the slide itself, not the screen (the lens will project the pointer onto the screen);

■ keep facing the audience, and don't be tempted to turn round and look at the screen while you are talking (this is bad body language and also makes you hard to hear).

Other commonly used visual aids include:

■ **computer-based presentations** such as PowerPoint – effective but require expertise to create

■ **35mm slide projectors** – professional but may be expensive

Slides can be produced quickly using special computer software and/or with the help of a photographer;

■ **video**, via TV screen or video projector – increasingly acceptable for showing locations, processes and short interviews

Hand-held cameras are widely available and easy to use, but there is a temptation to make video sequences too long

Several software packages are available and can reach a wider audience via a computer network.

Extension 2	Book	*How to be Twice as Smart*
	Author	Scott Witt
	Edition	1983
	Publisher	Reward Books
Extension 3	Book	*How to Win Friends and Influence People*
	Author	Dale Carnegie
	Edition	1984
	Publisher	Chancellor Press
Extension 4	Book	*NLP at Work*
	Author	Sue Knight
	Edition	2002
	Publisher	Nicholas Brealey Publishing
Extension 5	Book	*Body Talk – the skills of positive image*
	Author	Judi James
	Edition	1995
	Publisher	Spiro Press
Extension 6	Book	*Networking for Success*
	Author	Carol Harris
	Edition	2000
	Publisher	Oak Tree Press

These extensions can be taken up via your ILM Centre. They will either have them or will arrange that you have access to them.

4 Answers to self-assessment questions

Self-assessment 1 on pages 33–4

1   The hidden agenda is the feelings and attitudes that affect working relationships.

2   I **HEAR** and I forget.
    I see and I **REMEMBER**.
    I do and I **UNDERSTAND**.

3   If you know the nature of any objections to what you are going to say you will avoid being 'ambushed' and can deal with them in your own contribution.

4   Anxiety is the body's automatic reaction to a situation in which it believes that it is facing a serious threat.

5   A briefing or presentation should consist of:

- an introduction
- a main part
- a summary and conclusion

6   a Some things are easier to **COMMUNICATE** visually than in speech.
    b Visual aids help your listeners to **REMEMBER** the points you are making.
    c Visual aids make the whole presentation more **INTERESTING** and **CREDIBLE**.

7   The eight steps in carrying out a demonstration are:

1	Introduce the subject and describe what is required.
2	Explain why.
3	Explain when the new procedure is to be used.
4	Demonstrate how to carry out the procedure.
5	Ask team members to do it for themselves.
6	Correct and advise them where necessary.
7	Check understanding and competence.
8	If necessary, repeat steps 4 to 7.

8 The four questions to ask yourself are:

- what sort of people are in my audience?
- what are the **key** facts and feelings I want to pass on to them, i.e. what are my objectives?
- what do they know already?
- what are their current attitudes and feelings?

9 Rapport is a **good two-way relationship** between the speaker and the audience.

Self-assessment 2 on pages 60–1

1 We use our **SENSES** to build an image of what the people around us are like and how they will effect us.

2 Our five physical senses are sight, smell, hearing, taste and touch.

3 The communication process consists of a sender sending a **MESSAGE** to a receiver, and in return receiving **FEEDBACK**.

4 Feedback is of vital importance in the communication process because it tells the sender whether (a) the message has been understood, and (b) whether the desired outcome has been achieved.

5 Three techniques which will help you to ignore distractions when someone is speaking are:

- taking notes;
- playing mind games;
- using memory techniques.

6 The secret of active listening is to show that you are truly interested.

7

Type of listener	Their attention is internal	They are listening with their whole body
They think their own thoughts, make evaluations and judgements. They worry and concentrate on what just happened, what was just said or even what might happen next.	✓	
Their gaze is on the other person.		✓
They are in a state of curiosity. Their attention is entirely on the other person.		✓
Their language is likely to be 'I', 'me' centred.	✓	

8 You can judge the level of knowledge and language ability of someone about whom you know virtually nothing by:

■ asking them;
■ observing their body language.

9 A speaker's body language can:
a reduce the speaker's credibility by being distracting;
b weaken the message if it conflicts with it.

Self-assessment 3 on page 81

1 Networking can be defined as the creation and use of personal contacts for one's own **BENEFIT** or for the **BENEFIT** of a group.

2 In a network you use your contacts with other people to help both you and them to become more successful. A social group doesn't necessarily have any specific aim.

3 Networks can be classified as internal/external or knowledge networks/ mutual interest networks.

4 You could develop an internal network by:

■ establishing regular email correspondence with someone who has knowledge that will help you;
■ joining committees;
■ joining a company sports team.

5 A network designed specifically to benefit all members equally is a mutual interest network (MIN).

6 You should never ask advice from someone who usually charges for such information.

7 SWOT stands for strengths, weaknesses, opportunities and threats.

8 Yes. So long as you are on the same wavelength, it doesn't matter if you don't share their opinions.

5 Answers to activities

Activity 5 on page 8

There are several obvious things that you can do:

■ cut down the amount of information you provide;
■ slow down to a speed the listeners can cope with;
■ focus on a small number of issues;
■ organize what you are going to say so that it is easy to follow;
■ check frequently to make sure your audience is keeping up with you;
■ repeat and emphasize your key messages;
■ use visual aids and handouts.

Activity 26 on page 43

2 Paul has 'mismatch', 'internal', 'future' and 'towards' filters.

3 Jan has 'past', 'away from', 'match' and 'external' filters.

Activity 34 on page 55

Signals common in the UK that you might have listed include:

■ shaking the head to show disagreement;
■ beckoning with the hands;
■ waving to attract attention;
■ waving both hands from side to side to indicate 'stop';
■ pointing;
■ clapping;
■ shrugging the shoulders to indicate 'don't know' or 'don't care';
■ raising the arms to surrender;
■ shaking a fist to show anger.

6 Answers to the quick quiz

Answer 1 The main purpose of a briefing is to give information out and get information back.

Answer 2 When briefing people you don't know:

■ don't assume your listeners know as much as you do;
■ don't use language they might not understand;
■ don't give them too much information too quickly.

Answer 3   The steps involved in planning and preparing a briefing or presentation are:

Step	Action
1	Draft the objectives
2	List the content
3	Design the structure
4	Prepare the visual aids and demonstrations
5	Have a rehearsal

Answer 4   You should design the main part of the briefing or presentation first.

Answer 5   Before you begin your briefing or presentation, you should check that:

■ all your **VISUAL AIDS** are ready;
■ the **EQUIPMENT** is set up and working properly.

Answer 6   Techniques for getting your message across include the following:

1   Repeat the central message at least once.
2   Speak loudly and clearly.
3   Keep it short and simple.
4   Be assertive rather than aggressive.
5   Use words and phrases that you are confident the team members will understand.
6   Check that they understand.
7   Use eye contact.

Answer 7   The process through which the brain interprets information received from the senses is called 'perception'.

Answer 8   **'INTUITION'** is the sense that enables us to 'feel' what people are like.

Answer 9

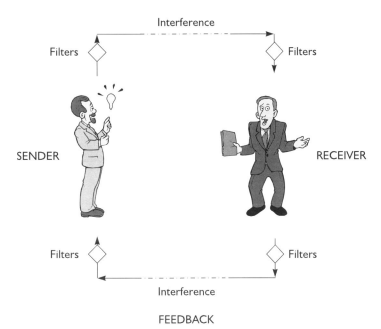

MESSAGE

Interference

Filters   Filters

SENDER   RECEIVER

Filters   Filters

Interference

FEEDBACK

Answer 10   Feedback tells the original sender whether:

- the message has got through;
- action, if any, has been or will be taken;
- the purpose has been achieved.

Answer 11   They are all 'flag' words that indicate that the speaker doesn't mean what he or she says.

Answer 12   Strengths, Weaknesses, Opportunities and Threats.

Answer 13   Three strategies you could use in forming an external network are:

- joining a special interest club;
- using internet chat rooms;
- developing social links with people in other organizations.

Answer 14   A **KNOWLEDGE NETWORK** is a ready-reference list of people who are willing and able to give you the information you need when you need it.

Answer 15   A **MUTUAL INTEREST NETWORK** is a group of people who enjoy sharing knowledge and enthusiasm for a particular topic.

7 Certificate

Completion of this certificate by an authorized person shows that you have worked through all the parts of this workbook and satisfactorily completed the assessments. The certificate provides a record of what you have done that may be used for exemptions or as evidence of prior learning against other nationally certificated qualifications.

Pergamon Flexible Learning and ILM are always keen to refine and improve their products. One of the key sources of information to help this process are people who have just used the product. If you have any information or views, good or bad, please pass these on.

INSTITUTE OF LEADERSHIP & MANAGEMENT

SUPER**SERIES**

Networking and Sharing Information

....

has satisfactorily completed this workbook

Name of signatory ....

Position ....

Signature ....

Date ....

Official stamp

Fourth Edition